CHILDREN'S MISCELLANY TOO

CHILDREN'S MISCELLANY 堛 *TOO*

More useless information that's essential to know

By Matthew Morgan and Samantha Barnes
Illustrated by Niki Catlow

chronicle books · san francisco

First published in the United States in 2006 by
Chronicle Books LLC.

Copyright © 2005 by Buster Books, U.K.
Originally published in Great Britain in 2005 by Buster Books,
an imprint of Michael O'Mara Books Limited, 9 Lion Yard,
Tremadoc Road, London, SW4 7NQ.
All rights reserved.

Typeset in Langer.
Manufactured in China.

Library of Congress Cataloging-in-Publication Data
Morgan, Matthew.
Children's miscellany too : more useless information that's essential
to know / by Matthew Morgan and Samantha Barnes ;
illustrated by Niki Catlow.
p. cm.
ISBN-13: 978-0-8118-5639-3
ISBN-10: 0-8118-5639-9
1. Curiosities and wonders — Juvenile literature.
2. Handbooks, vade-mecums, etc. — Juvenile literature.
I. Barnes, Samantha. II. Catlow, Niki. III. Title.
AG243.M666 2006
031.02 — dc22
2006007151

Distributed in Canada by Raincoast Books
9050 Shaughnessy Street, Vancouver, British Columbia V6P 6E5

10 9 8 7 6 5 4 3 2 1

Chronicle Books LLC
85 Second Street, San Francisco, California 94105

www.chroniclekids.com

CONTENTS

Lifetime averages	11
Some important state facts	11
Cryptids	12
Double-jointedness	12
Disgusting and dangerous plants	13
Cool transport	13
Things to dress up as when running a marathon	14
How to get rid —*hic*— of hiccups	14
The afterlife	14
Funny bones	15
Yuor azamnig mnid	15
Wise words	16
Archenemies of superheroes	16
Morse code alphabet	17
Down the hatch	17
Things that have rained from the sky	18
What green means	18
Who is that relative?	18
Diseases you really don't want to catch	19
The best way to make yourself dizzy	19
The origins of the salute	20
Seven modern world wonders	20
Seven natural world wonders	20
The five stages of sleep	21
Rubber bands	21
Chicken flight	21
How to hypnotize a chicken	22
Why boys are better than girls	22
Why girls are better than boys	22
What kind of maniac are you?	23
Early brain surgery	23
The silent alphabet	24
The Mozart effect	24
When should you sneeze?	25
Longest sneezing bout	25
Elbow	25
Computer bytes	25
What is air?	25
Pointless instructions	26
What to do if zombies attack	27
True or false?	27
What is a googol?	27
Phineas Gage	28
Men who were women	28
Would you rather . . .	29
Vegetables that are in fact fruits	29
The Statue of Liberty	30
Spiders' webs	30

CONTENTS

Things to put in a
  time capsule 30
Very strange sports 31
Dogs' work 31
Things you wish you
  didn't know about
  the Romans 32
Names from
  Harry Potter 33
Capital cities you might
  not know 33
How to make a paper
  water balloon 34
Secrets of snot 36
Egyptian gods and
  their animal forms 36
The Simpsons 37
Strawberries 37
Bits of brain 38
Language families 38
What to do in an
  earthquake 39
Ten books 39
Film facts 39
The amount of DNA you
  share with . . . 40
Clandestine government
  organizations 40
Light, sound, and
  electricity in animals 41
The meaning of dreams 42
Strange swallowings 42
Things that have claws 43

Fire talk 43
*The Great Fire of
  London* 43
King Arthur's Knights of
  the Round Table 44
Names celebrities have
  given their children 44
Chocolate timeline 45
Funny facial hairstyles 46
Three cups trick 47
Items not allowed in your
  carry-on luggage 47
Lord Oxford's fart 47
Extreme Earth 48
Skin deep 48
Mythical creatures 49
Riddles 50
Micro or nano? 50
Real-life pirates 51
What do toothless
  animals eat? 51
I invented it. No, I
  invented it 52
What yellow means 52
How to write a haiku 53
Excuse me 53
Incredible insects 54
*Oldest playable
  musical instrument* 54
Yy u r yy u b i c
  u r yy 4 me 54
Famous Nobel Prize
  winners 55

CONTENTS

Real alternatives to
toilet paper 55
How many magpies? 56
Message not always
fully understood 56
Farts 56
Siege engines 57
Strange remedies 58
Things that harm the
planet 58
How to fly a helicopter 59
Things that shrink 59
Sporting losers 60
The worst place to . . . 60
The rhyming
weather forecast 61
Things we use trees for 62
Shakespearean insults 62
Abbreviations 63
Famous real-life dogs 63
Famous real-life cats 63
Fortune teller 64
Vitamin deficiencies 66
*Orange, purple, and
silver* 66
Top five all-time
worldwide box-
office hits 67
The Chinese calendar 67
Phrenology 68
Causes of
crop circles: theories 69

Body appendages 69
Animals that can
change color 69
Space firsts 70
Are you in proportion? 71
Onomatopoeic words 71
The Great Pyramid of
Khufu (or Cheops)
at Giza 71
The Enigma machine 72
What red means 72
Who is that celebrity? 73
One hundred and one 73
Survivors of
assassination attempts 73
An alchemist's recipe
for gold 74
"Facts" that are not true 75
Animals that
metamorphose 75
Possible or impossible? 76
What do you get when
you cross . . . 76
Great warriors 77
How fast is the world
spinning? 77
Silly signs 78
The phonetic alphabet 78
Criminal masterminds? 79
Something fishy 80
I feel the need, the
need for speed 80

CONTENTS

How to turn your watch into a compass 81

Four-year-olds 81

The origins of text messaging 82

Emoticons 82

Real newspaper headlines 83

Cartoon cats 83

Cartoon dogs 83

Who's the tallest? 84

Reds, blues, and greens 84

Ways to choose who is "it" 85

What does your handwriting say about you? 85

Postage stamps 86

Things that are fun to say 86

Like which animal? 87

Inventions that didn't make it 87

The predictions of Nostradamus 88

Three terrifying people 88

Big birds 89

Fun houses 89

Hairy humans 90

Extreme ironing 90

Ten famous volcanoes 91

Which doorway? 91

A baby in Florida 91

Medieval torture instruments 92

Funny place names around the world 93

Richest women in the world 93

For your address book 94

How long do your cells live? 94

The 12 labors of Hercules 95

2B or not 2B? 96

Pigpen 97

Insect grub 97

Your birthday 97

Jaws 98

Days of the week 98

Absence excuse notes 99

Super powers 99

Statues 99

Vaccines in fruits 99

They say it's going to rain if . . . 100

Opposites 100

Why you don't want to mess with creepy crawlies 100

More "facts" that are not true 101

City anagrams 101

Imposters 102

CONTENTS

Highest-earning fictional characters 102
The signs of madness 103
Card trick 103
Say what you see 104
Hottest, coldest, driest, wettest 105
Your brain 105
Locusts 105
The Olympic Games 106
What's black and white and red all over? 107
Famous ghosts 107
Mixing color 108
The fate of the children in Charlie and the Chocolate Factory 108
Finger fun 109
What teachers really mean 109
Why is the sky blue? 110
Everyday inventions 110
Countries with the most tractors per person 111
Annoying things teachers always say 111
Music genres 111
Names of the months 112
Seven spells from Harry Potter 113
How to fake a smile 113
The Chair of Truth 114
Rabbit or duck? 114
Sweat 115
A Roman banquet set menu 115
Ten Grand Prix Formula 1 Champions 116
Toilet paper 116
The five deadliest places on Earth 117
Languages of wider communication 117
Art movements 118
Homemade invisible ink 118
Moons of Jupiter 118
Unidentified flying objects 119
Tangrams 120
The longest place names in the world 121
Ground-to-air code 121
Five famous hoaxes 122
Time flies 122
Five ways to de-smell your sneakers 123
Celebrity dragons 123
What animals say 124
What blue means 124
Rainbows—the truth and the lies 125
Name that band 125
You are now . . . 126

LIFETIME AVERAGES

Time spent on the toilet..6 months
Time spent eating..3 years
Time spent waiting for things..3 years
Time spent talking...10 years
Time spent sleeping..22 years
Number of times fingers bent and straightened...................25 million
Number of smells remembered...10,000
Distance traveled on foot.....................14,000 mi. (22,500 km)
Length of hair grown................................621 mi. (1,000 km)
Volume of tears shed................................14.3 gal. (65 l)
Weight of skin shed..................................105 lb. (47.5 kg)
Number of balloons you could fill with exhaled air.............14 million
Volume of blood pumped around body.........100,000 gal. (380,000 l)
Number of cells produced......................................750,000 billion

SOME IMPORTANT STATE FACTS

The cheeseburger was invented in Colorado.
New Jersey has more toxic waste dumps than any other state.
Dog mushing is the official state sport of Alaska.
Wisconsin's Mount Horeb houses the world's largest
mustard collection.
There are more turkeys in California than in any other state.

CRYPTIDS

(Animals that have been rumored but not proven to exist.)

ORANG PENDEK
A mysteriously human-like ape from Sumatra covered in thick dark hair, with a long mane and a hairless brown face.

MONGOLIAN DEATH WORM
A 4-foot-long red worm from the Gobi desert that can kill instantly from several feet away, by shooting poison or electric currents at its prey.

TRUNKO
A whale-sized furry sea mammal with an elephantine trunk, said to have washed up on the coast of South Africa.

CHUPACABRA
A bloodsucking beast from Central America that walks on two legs, has large black eyes, and attacks goats and cattle.

THUNDERBIRD
A huge bird with a wingspan of over 20 ft. (6 m) that is said to have appeared in a photograph in the Wild West but has since disappeared.

SUCURIJU GIGANTE
A giant anaconda around 40 ft. (12 m) long that lives in the Amazon rainforest.

DOUBLE-JOINTEDNESS

One in every 20 people is double-jointed in some way. The medical term for it is "joint hypermobility," meaning that a person's joint has been formed in such a way as to allow for extra movement—it's actually nothing to do with having "double" of anything. If you have these very flexible joints you might be able to:

Touch your wrist with the thumb of the same hand.

Bend your elbows backward.

Lie on your stomach with your feet touching your head.

Bend over and put your shoulders between your knees.

Join your hands behind your back and lift them over your head without letting go.

DISGUSTING AND DANGEROUS PLANTS

STINKY FLOWERS
The rafflesia and titan arum plants smell horribly of rotting meat.

PITCHER PLANTS
This plant has leaves in the shape of tubular jugs. Insects fall in and cannot climb out.

FLYPAPER
The sundew has sticky hairs on its leaves, which trap insects that the plant then digests.

VENUS FLYTRAP
Has a hinged leaf with two spined lobes like scary jaws. The lobes snap shut on any small beast that might venture into the "mouth," and do not reopen until the creature has been digested.

STRANGLER
This type of fig tree produces roots above ground that wrap themselves around other trees . . . or whatever else gets in their way.

COOL TRANSPORT

Skateboards • Rollerskates • Ice skates • Hoppity balls

Pogo sticks • Bicycles • Tricycles • Unicycles

————THINGS TO DRESS UP AS———— WHEN RUNNING A MARATHON

Gorilla • Sumo wrestler • Rhinoceros • Cottage • Chicken
Viking longboat • Salmon (start at the finish line and run
"upstream") • Deep-sea diver (including lead boots)

———HOW TO GET RID—*HIC*—OF HICCUPS———

Bend over at the waist and drink water from the farther side
of a glass (that is, with your chin stuck in the glass).

Hold your breath for at least a minute.

Try to swallow a spoonful of peanut butter.

Pull hard on your tongue.

Place a spoonful of sugar at the back of your tongue; repeat
two to three times as necessary.

Suck on a piece of fresh lemon.

Take a deep breath and hold it while squeezing your stomach
muscles as hard as possible.

Think of the ugliest person you have ever seen.

————————THE AFTERLIFE————————

RELIGION	FOR THE GOOD	FOR THE WICKED
Ancient Greek	Elysium	Hades
Ancient Egyptian	Yaru	Eaten by Devourer
Christianity	Heaven	Hell
Islam	Paradise	Jahannam
Judaism	Garden of Eden	She'ol/Gehenna
Buddhism	Nirvana	Reincarnation as a worm

FUNNY BONES

Number of bones babies have...300

Number of bones adults have..206

Number of bones in hands and feet..106

Number of bones in head...22

Smallest bone.......................................Stirrup bone, ear (0.1 in., 2.5 mm)

Longest bone................Femur, thigh (a quarter of a person's height)

Hardest bone............................Petrous temporal bone, base of skull

Only bone not connected to another............Hyoid, base of tongue

YUOR AZAMNIG MNID

Sceitnsits hvae dsicveored taht the hmuan biran is so uesd to raednig taht it deosn't mtater waht oredr the letetrs are in, as lnog as you mkae srue the frist and lsat ltteers are in the rhgit pclae. Tihs is bcuease we raed the wlhoe wrod, rthaer tahn ecah ltteer. In fcat, eevn thguoh the mdilde leettrs are jmulbed up, yuor biarn is pobrbaly cveelr eognuh to raed tihs wouthit too mcuh truolbe.

─────WISE WORDS─────

Don't pick on your sister when she's holding a hockey stick.

If you want a kitten, start out by asking for a horse.

If you get a bad school report, wait until your mom's on the phone to show it to her.

When your dad is mad at you and asks "Do I *look* stupid?" don't answer him.

When you want something expensive, ask your grandparents.

Never tell your little sister that you're not going to do what your mom told you to do.

Always look busy with homework when your mom shows up with a broom or vacuum cleaner.

Never dare your little brother to paint the family car.

─────ARCHENEMIES OF SUPERHEROES─────

Lex Luthor	Superman
The Joker	Batman
The Green Goblin	Spider-Man
The Cheetah	Wonder Woman
Black Adam	Captain Marvel
Duke Nukem	Captain Planet
Oil Can Harry	Mighty Mouse

MORSE CODE ALPHABET

A	.–	H	....	O	– – –	V	...–
B	–...	I	..	P	.– –.	W	.– –
C	–.–.	J	.– – –	Q	– –.–	X	–..–
D	–..	K	–.–	R	.–.	Y	–.– –
E	.	L	.–..	S	...	Z	– –..
F	..–.	M	– –	T	–		
G	– –.	N	–.	U	..–		

DOWN THE HATCH

Keep a piece of bread in your mouth for a few minutes and after a short while you'll notice a sweet taste. That is the beginning of digestion, as enzymes in your saliva begin to dissolve the food and break down the carbohydrates into sugar.

The next step is when you swallow the food—down it goes into the stomach—a churning pool of hydrochloric acid, enzymes, and other fluids that break the food down further. If you could separate that acid from the enzymes and other fluids, it would be strong enough to dissolve iron nails. (Luckily your stomach protects itself with a bicarbonate lining.)

Then the food is pushed into the 18 ft. (5 m) long (longer in an adult) coiled-up small intestine, and is squeezed along the length of it. More digestive juices—from the pancreas and liver—pour onto the food particles before at last they are pushed out of the small intestine.

By now the body has extracted from the bits of food all that it needs in the way of nutrients, and the food is in the large intestine (three times wider than the small, but only about 5 ft., or 1.5 m, long). There, any remaining water is sucked out of the food and it descends as a lump of brown waste to join more brown waste at the bottom of the large intestine. And there it waits until . . .

. . . the owner of the intestines hurries off to the bathroom.

——THINGS THAT HAVE RAINED FROM THE SKY——

Frogs	Squid
Hermit crabs	Jellyfish
Worms	Corn
Sardines	Colored rain
Catfish	Baby alligators
Butterflies	Beer cans

——————WHAT GREEN MEANS——————

Growth • Spring • New life • Youth • Inexperience • Hope
Prosperity • Relaxation • Passivity • Receptivity • Harmony
Reassurance • Safety • Envy • Jealousy

——————WHO IS THAT RELATIVE?——————

Half-brother or sister.................................Shares one parent with you

Stepmom/dad..Your parent's wife/husband

Stepbrother/sister...Your stepmom/dad's child

First cousin...Your aunt or uncle's child

Second cousin...Your parent's cousin's child

Third cousin..............................Your grandparent's cousin's grandchild

First cousin once removed......................................Your parent's cousin
OR your cousin's child

First cousin twice removed.........................Your grandparent's cousin
OR your cousin's grandchild

Second cousin once removed..............Your parent's second cousin
OR your second cousin's child

—DISEASES YOU REALLY DON'T WANT TO CATCH—

YELLOW FEVER
50 percent of sufferers die—caught from mosquitoes. Starts with a fever, vomiting, and sore eyes. Death from organ failure.

LASSA FEVER
20 percent die if left untreated—caught from rats. Death from brain inflammation and bleeding.

BUBONIC PLAGUE
60 percent die if left untreated—starts with a sore throat, fever, and headache. Leads to abscesses, gangrene, and fits.

NECROTIZING FASCIITIS
50 percent die—caught from other people. Death by flesh-eating killer bug unless all infected areas are cut out.

EBOLA VIRUS
50 percent die—starts with a rash, fever, and headache. Death from bleeding and coma.

CHOLERA
50 percent die if left untreated—caught from poop-infected water. Begins with diarrhea and vomiting. Death from dehydration and organ failure.

MARBURG DISEASE
60 percent die—caught from monkeys. Death from kidney, liver, lung, or brain failure.

RABIES
100 percent die if left untreated—result of being bitten by an infected animal. Leads to madness and inflammation of the brain.

——THE BEST WAY TO MAKE YOURSELF DIZZY——

Bend over and hold your left ankle with your right hand, then spin counter-clockwise.

THE ORIGINS OF THE SALUTE

In Roman times, when assassination and murder were rife, or even well before, it was the custom to greet someone by holding up an empty hand—to show that you were not carrying a weapon.

Medieval knights would similarly show an empty hand as an indication that they meant no harm. They would also lift up the visors of their helmets to show their face.

The removal of a helmet or other headgear indoors was a sign of respect which, applied to hats of all kinds, has been carried on through the centuries.

—SEVEN MODERN— WORLD WONDERS

The Aswan High Dam

The Channel Tunnel

The Eiffel Tower

The Golden Gate Bridge

The Panama Canal

The Statue of Liberty

The Trans-Siberian Railway

—SEVEN NATURAL— WORLD WONDERS

The Northern Lights

Mount Everest

Uluru (Ayers Rock)

The Great Barrier Reef

Victoria Falls

The Grand Canyon

The Icelandic Hot Springs

—————————THE FIVE STAGES OF SLEEP—————————

LIGHT SLEEP: During this period you are half-awake and half-asleep. For about 10 minutes you can easily be awakened. People can take "cat naps" with their eyes open without even being aware of it.

TRUE SLEEP: This lasts for about 20 minutes. While you are asleep your body produces large amounts of growth hormones that help repair or replace damaged cells, and chemicals important to the immune system—thus speeding up healing and keeping you healthy.

DEEP SLEEP: Your brainwave patterns slow down. The slower the brainwaves, the deeper the sleep. Sleep gives your brain a chance to organize the previous day's events and file away memories. Lack of sleep makes you irritable, forgetful, inattentive, unable to make judgments, uncoordinated, and more likely to fall ill. Severe sleep deprivation causes paranoia, delusions, and hallucinations.

DEEPER SLEEP: Your breathing becomes slow and rhythmic, and your muscles are barely active.

REM (RAPID EYE MOVEMENT): 70 to 90 minutes after you fall asleep you start dreaming. Your eyes move about, your brain becomes very active, and your breathing rate and blood pressure rise; your muscles relax so much that your body seems unable to move. Most dreams last 6 to 10 minutes, but can last longer. The record is 150 minutes. Happy dreams are more common; any nightmares you might have usually come toward morning.

Rubber bands last longer if you keep them in the fridge.

The longest recorded flight of a chicken is 13 seconds.

———————HOW TO HYPNOTIZE A CHICKEN———————

Rest assured that no chicken is hurt during this; not even its dignity is shaken (unless you ask it to run around like a human when it is in the trance)! This is one of several ways to lull a chicken into a stupor— just make sure you are gentle and quiet.

1. Place the chicken on a table, laying it on its side with one wing under its body. Hold it down gently with its head flat on the surface.

2. With one finger from your free hand repeatedly trace a straight line, about 1 ft. (30 cm) long, in front of the bird's eyes —outward from its beak-tip and along the table. Alternatively, take a piece of chalk (a color that contrasts with the surface) and draw a 1 ft. (30 cm) line from the beak-tip out in front of the bird. Hold the chicken still for a bit as it stares ahead along the line.

Soon the chicken will be in a hypnotic trance. How long it remains in that trance varies from seconds to hours. But any sudden movement or noise will bring the bird to and, with a squawk of surprise, it'll be up and on its way.

—WHY BOYS ARE— BETTER THAN GIRLS	—WHY GIRLS ARE— BETTER THAN BOYS
Boys don't mind if they run out of clean pants. It is easy for boys to pee outside.	Girls don't have to smell their clothes to know if they're clean. Girls never miss the toilet.

──────WHAT KIND OF MANIAC ARE YOU?──────

(Maniac: a person who is obsessed with something)

Pyromaniac	Fire
Balletomaniac	Ballet
Islomaniac	Islands
Egomaniac	Yourself
Bibliomaniac	Books
Dipsomaniac	Alcohol
Anthomaniac	Flowers
Graphomaniac	Writing
Dromomaniac	Running
Monomaniac	One thing
Mythomaniac	Lying

──────────EARLY BRAIN SURGERY──────────

Trepanning was a medical practice used as long ago as 7000 BC to treat bad headaches, head injuries, seizures, and possession by evil spirits. A hole was cut into the skull using a stone ax or a knife. As there was no anesthetic, the patients were either knocked out or held down to prevent them from running away. How well the surgery worked is debatable, but in a great many cases the patient survived and was presumably restored to health, as the holes in skulls found by archaeologists can be seen to have partially repaired themselves. Trepanning continued to be practiced in ancient Egypt, Greece, and Rome, through medieval times, and beyond. And it is still practiced today, generally in cases where there is bleeding between the brain and the skull, as this can produce too much pressure on the brain and even cause death. Afterward, the hole is fitted with a neat metal disc in place of the removed bone.

THE SILENT ALPHABET

A as in bread

B as in debt

C as in indictment
(pronounced "in-dite-ment")

D as in handkerchief

E as in give

F as in halfpenny
(pronounced "hay-penny")

G as in gnaw

H as in hour

I as in friend

J as in rijsttafel (a cold buffet
pronounced "rice-taffel")

K as in know

L as in the first *l* in colonel

M as the first *m* in mnemonic

N as in autumn

O as in people

P as in psalm

Q as in Colquhoun
(a Scottish surname
pronounced "Co-hoon")

R as in February

S as in island

T as in castle

U as in guard

V as in Milngavie
(a Scottish place name
pronounced "Mull-ga'i")

W as in wrong

X as in Sioux
(pronounced "Soo")

Y as in key

Z as in rendezvous

THE MOZART EFFECT

The Mozart Effect is a phrase used to mean that music has a beneficial effect on health, happiness, and education. This seems a reasonable assessment—except that some people got over-excited by scientists' reports, and interpreted them to mean that listening to Mozart magically makes you smarter. For the last ten years or more the Mozart Effect has been argued about. There is no reason to believe that listening to Mozart will raise your overall IQ—but you might well find that listening to many kinds of music makes you feel happier, calmer, and less stressed, so you can think more clearly and work better.

---WHEN SHOULD YOU SNEEZE?---

Sneeze on Monday,
sneeze for danger;

Sneeze on Tuesday,
kiss a stranger;

Sneeze on Wednesday,
get a letter;

Sneeze on Thursday,
something better;

Sneeze on Friday,
sneeze for sorrow;

Sneeze on Saturday,
see your sweetheart tomorrow;

Sneeze on Sunday, your safety seek, for the Devil will
have you the whole of the week.

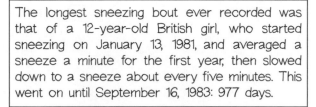

> The longest sneezing bout ever recorded was
> that of a 12-year-old British girl, who started
> sneezing on January 13, 1981, and averaged a
> sneeze a minute for the first year, then slowed
> down to a sneeze about every five minutes. This
> went on until September 16, 1983: 977 days.

> It's impossible to lick your elbow.

-COMPUTER BYTES-	---WHAT IS AIR?---
1 byte = 8 binary digits (bits)	78 percent nitrogen
1 kilobyte (KB) = 1,024 bytes	21 percent oxygen
1 megabyte (MB) = 1,024KB	.03 percent carbon dioxide
1 gigabyte (GB) = 1,024MB	.07 percent other

POINTLESS INSTRUCTIONS

On a blanket from Taiwan:
"Not to be used as
protection from a tornado."

*On a helmet-mounted
mirror used by U.S. cyclists:*
"Remember, objects in
the mirror are actually
behind you."

*On the bottle top of
a flavored milk drink:*
"After opening, keep upright."

On a bag of chips:
"You could be a winner.
No purchase necessary.
Details inside."

On a bag of peanuts:
"Warning—contains nuts."

On a Korean kitchen knife:
"Warning: keep out
of children."

*On a string of Chinese-
made Christmas lights:*
"For indoor or outdoor
use only."

*On a Japanese
food processor:*
"Not to be used for the
other use."

*On the bottom of a
tiramisu dessert box:*
"Do not turn upside down."

On a Superman costume:
"Wearing this garment does
not enable you to fly."

──────────WHAT TO DO IF ZOMBIES ATTACK──────────

Act fast—zombies multiply very quickly.

Dress in protective bite-proof clothing (e.g., leather).

Listen to the news to find out which areas are safe and which are most dangerous.

Rescue as many survivors as possible—there's safety in numbers.

Make sure none of the survivors have secretly been bitten—they may become zombies and turn on you later.

Zombies are slow, so run for it.

Zombies are also stupid, so confuse them by changing direction and creating diversions.

Make sure you have plenty of food and water (a supermarket makes an ideal shelter).

Lock all doors and windows and pile heavy objects against them for extra security.

Remember, zombies can only be killed by destroying their brain, so don't waste energy fighting them.

> The following sentence is false. The preceding sentence is true. Are these sentences true or false?

──────────────WHAT IS A GOOGOL?──────────────

A googol is 1 followed by 100 zeroes.

Because this takes a long time to write and it is easy to lose count of all those zeroes, we say: 10 to the power of 100. This is written 10^{100}.

A googolplex is 10 to the power of a googol—or 10 to the power of 10 to the power of 100. This is written $(10^{10})^{100}$. It is not a number for which there is much demand.

PHINEAS GAGE

Phineas Gage was a railroad worker. On September 13, 1848, he was packing some gunpowder into a hole with a long steel rod when the gunpowder went off. The steel bar went straight through his head . . . and he lived. His doctor patched him up, and he was fine—he could still walk and talk and do math; he had all of his memories—but his *personality* had changed. Phineas was suddenly an angrier, more irrational person. He had lost the ability to get along with other people.

His case fundamentally changed the way doctors think about the brain.

MEN WHO WERE WOMEN

GEORGE ELIOT (1819–1876)
Actually named Mary Ann Evans, this novelist used a male pen name so that her work would be taken seriously.

ANNE BONNEY AND MARY READ (early 1700s)
These pirates disguised themselves as men because at that time sailors believed it was bad luck to have a woman onboard ship.

LE BLANC (1776–1831)
Sophie Germain presented a mathematics paper that was so impressive the professor sought out this "student." The professor was amazed to find that "he" was a young Frenchwoman and entirely self-taught.

JAMES BARRY (1795–1865)
A surgeon in the British Army, James was discovered to have been a woman only at "his" death.

————WOULD YOU RATHER . . .————

. . . have your legs on backward or live with
a second head?

. . . be hideously ugly or horribly smelly?

. . . own a hamster as big as a dog or a dog as
small as a hamster?

. . . squeak when you walk or blow bubbles when you talk?

. . . be three feet taller or three feet shorter?

. . . use a chainshaw as a toothbrush or a chainsaw
for a nail file?

. . . talk like Yoda or breathe like Darth Vader for
the rest of your life?

. . . have a body covered with scales or a
body covered with fur?

. . . be covered in molasses and stung to death by bees
or be covered in honey and eaten by bears?

. . . be able to fly or be able to travel through time?

. . . have a theme tune for all of your actions for the
rest of your life or have no reflection?

————VEGETABLES THAT ARE IN FACT FRUITS————

Tomatoes • Cucumbers • Eggplants • Zucchini • Peppers

Chilies • Avocados • Squash • Pumpkins • Peapods

───────────THE STATUE OF LIBERTY───────────

On the base of the Statue of Liberty is inscribed a poem by Emma Lazarus entitled "The New Colossus":

Not like the brazen giant of Greek fame,
With conquering limbs astride from land to land;
Here at our sea-washed, sunset gates shall stand
A mighty woman with a torch, whose flame
Is the imprisoned lightning, and her name
Mother of Exiles. From her beacon-hand
Glows world-wide welcome; her mild eyes command
The air-bridged harbor that twin cities frame,
"Keep, ancient lands, your storied pomp!" cries she
With silent lips. "Give me your tired, your poor,
Your huddled masses yearning to breathe free,
The wretched refuse of your teeming shore,
Send these, the homeless, tempest-tossed to me,
I lift my lamp beside the golden door!"

The Statue of Liberty would wear a women's shoe size 879.

A spider's web is made of two types of thread, one sticky and the other not. The spider makes the non-sticky spokes first, then builds the sticky spiral part onto the frame. The spider walks on the spokes and avoids the sticky strands.

───────THINGS TO PUT IN A TIME CAPSULE───────

A lock of your hair
Today's newspaper
A picture of you and your best friend
A description of what you think the future will be like
An item connected with your favorite hobby
A CD with your favorite song on it

VERY STRANGE SPORTS

Cheese rolling, England and Italy
Cup stacking, USA
Wife carrying, Finland and Estonia
Zorbing (rolling around in an inflatable sphere), New Zealand
Cowpat tossing, Oklahoma, USA
Bog snorkeling, international
Cockroach racing, Australia
Biplane wing walking, international

DOGS' WORK

HERDING	HUNTING	GUARDING	RETRIEVING
Afghan hound	Beagle	Doberman	Labrador
Alsatian	Borzoi	Lhasa apso	Poodle
Border collie	Chow	Schipperke	Curly-coated retriever
Puli	Greyhound	Bernese mountain dog	Golden retriever
Samoyed	Jack Russell		

THINGS YOU WISH YOU DIDN'T KNOW — ABOUT THE ROMANS

They had ten-seater communal toilets. As there was no toilet paper, they shared a wet sponge on a stick.

They didn't use soap. They covered their bodies with oil and scraped off the dirt.

They washed their clothes (and sometimes their hair) in urine to get the grease out.

They cleaned their teeth with a mixture of powdered mouse brains, honey, and ashes made by burning dog's teeth.

Although it was illegal, some Romans sold their children as slaves if they didn't like them.

When they ate too much, they would be sick in special rooms called vomitoriums, and then come back to carry on eating.

Roman doctors were trained to ignore the screams of soldiers, and would amputate their arms or legs without any painkillers.

─────────NAMES FROM HARRY POTTER─────────

Albus Dumbledore	*Albus* means white in Latin; *dumbledore* means bumblebee in Old English.
Minerva McGonagall	Minerva is the Roman goddess of wisdom; the Scottish last name McGonagall comes from an old Celtic word meaning valor.
Remus Lupin	Remus is a character in Roman mythology who was raised by a wolf; *lupin* is from the Roman *lupus*, which means wolf.
Sirius Black	Sirius is the name of a star also known as the Dog Star.
Peter Pettigrew	*Petti* is from a French root meaning small, so *Pettigrew* means "grows small"; *Peter* means the same thing.
Dolores Umbridge	*Dolores* is from a Spanish root meaning pain; *umbridge* is a variation on the word *umbrage*, which relates to resentment or anger.
Voldemort	In French, *voldemort* could be translated to mean "escape from death."
Avada Kedavra	An Aramaic phrase that means "may it be destroyed."
Crucio	In Latin, *crucio* means "I torture."
Imperio	A variation on the Latin *impero*, which means "I command."

─────────CAPITAL CITIES YOU MIGHT NOT KNOW─────────

Pago Pago, American Samoa • Nuuk, Greenland
Nuku'alofa, Tonga • Dalap-Uliga-Darrit, Marshall Islands
Thimphu, Bhutan • Roseau, Dominica • The Valley, Anguilla
Nouakchott, Mauritania • Ouagadougou, Burkina Faso
Podgorica, Montenegro

──HOW TO MAKE A PAPER WATER BALLOON──

Start with a square piece of paper.

1. Fold in half vertically. Unfold. Fold in half horizontally. Unfold.

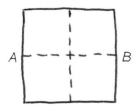

2. Turn over. Fold in half diagonally in both directions. Unfold.

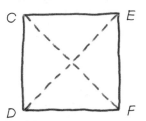

3. Fold along creases so that A and B touch each other.

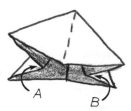

4. Fold C and E up so that they touch G. Repeat on the other side with D and F.

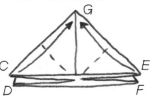

5. Fold the side corners into the center. Repeat on the other side.

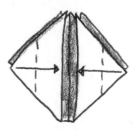

6. Fold the little top corners into the center. Repeat on the other side.

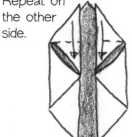

7. Now fold the little triangles you've just made over the big triangles and unfold. Repeat on the other side.

8. Using the creases made in step 7, tuck the small triangles into the pockets of the big triangles. Repeat on the other side.

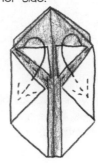

9. To inflate the water balloon, blow into the hole at the bottom.

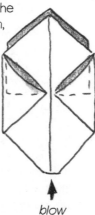

blow

When it is finished, your water balloon should look like this. Fill it up and give your friends a good soaking!

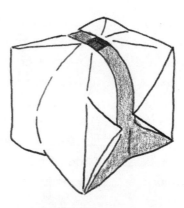

---SECRETS OF SNOT---

Snot is mucus—a slimy substance produced by plants and animals.

Snot keep things running smoothly, like engine oil in a car.

Snot traps any dust and objects (including small insects) that might go up your nostrils.

Boogers are dried-up, dust- and germ-filled bits of snot.

Sneezing blasts out snot at 100 mph (160 kph).

When you have a cold your body produces extra snot to rid itself of invading viruses.

When your snot turns into nasty-colored thick mucus it is usually because an infection has taken hold and your body is fighting against it.

---EGYPTIAN GODS AND THEIR ANIMAL FORMS---

Amun....................The Supreme God....................Ram
Anubis....................God of the Dead....................Jackal
Bast....................Daughter of The Sun God Ra....................Cat
Horus....................God of the Sky....................Falcon
Mut....................Queen of All Gods....................Vulture
Sekhmet....................Goddess of War....................Lioness
Seth....................God of Chaos and Evil....................Monster
Thoth....................God of the Moon and Wisdom....................Ibis
Hathor....................Goddess of Love and Nurture....................Cow

THE SIMPSONS

"Doh" now appears in the online version of the *Oxford English Dictionary.*

Matt Groening named the characters after his own family: his father is named Homer, his mother is Margaret (Marge), one sister is Lisa, another is Maggie. Bart is an anagram of *brat,* which is a rhyming reference to himself, Matt.

Matt Groening named his sons, born in 1991 and 1993, Homer and Abe.

Look at Homer from the side and you can see that the zigzag of his hair forms an M for Matt, and his ear forms a G for Groening.

In one episode Lisa gives her email address as smartgirl63_\@yahoo.com.

In 2004 Marge was voted the United Kingdom's favorite mother.

Among the business names of Springfield are a law firm called I Can't Believe It's A Law Firm!; a toy store called J. R. R. Toykins; a pastry shop called The French Confection; a seafood restaurant called The Fryin' Dutchman; and the comic book store, Android's Dungeon.

Krusty the Clown's real name is Herschel Schmoikel Krustofski.

In one episode, two area codes are given that would locate half of Springfield in Missouri and half in Puerto Rico (an island)! Elsewhere, we are told that Springfield is 678 mi. (1,091.14 km) from Mexico City and 2,653 mi. (4,269.59 km) from Orlando, Florida—an impossibility.

Springfield's official motto is "Corruptus in Extremis," and the motto of the mystery state in which it lies is "Not just another state."

Strawberries have more vitamin C than oranges.

BITS OF BRAIN

Your brain is divided into three main parts:

1. The brain stem to the back of your head, at the bottom, which deals with automatic actions like breathing and digestion.

2. The cerebellum at the back, which controls and coordinates day-to-day actions such as walking.

3. The cerebrum at the front, which plans and controls movements; interprets the messages it receives from your eyes, ears, tongue, fingertips, etc.; and remembers, thinks, and solves problems. The right-hand side is more involved in creative and artistic activities; the left-hand side is used for logical or mathematical processes.

LANGUAGE FAMILIES

Number of languages in the world..over 6,000

Number of language families..12

Biggest language family...Indo-European

Second biggest language family...Sino-Tibetan

Most difficult language to learn..Basque

————————WHAT TO DO IN AN EARTHQUAKE————————

Stay indoors. Stand away from windows, mirrors,
and other glass.

Take shelter under a table or desk. This will protect you from
falling objects and give you breathing space. Otherwise,
standing in the corner of a room or in a doorframe is safest.

Lower-level floors are safer than higher ones, but getting in an
elevator or trying to run downstairs is dangerous.

If you are outside, lie flat on the ground away from
tall trees and buildings.

If you are near the sea, get to higher ground as a tidal wave
may follow the earthquake.

If you have ten books, you could arrange
them 3,628,800 ways on your shelf.

————————————FILM FACTS————————————

George Lucas originally had trouble getting funding for *Star
Wars* because most studios thought that people wouldn't
bother going to see it. In fact, it won six Academy Awards and
was an enormous box-office hit.

The MGM lion, Leo, has been played by a number of lions,
among them animals called Slats, Jackie, and Tanner.

The real name of Toto the dog in *The Wizard of Oz* was
Terry—her salary was $125 per week. Judy Garland, who
played Dorothy, earned $500 per week.

India's movie industry, Bollywood, is the largest in the world
and produces over 800 movies a year. Hollywood only
produces half that number.

5,247 lb. (2,380 kg) of modeling clay was used in the making
of *Chicken Run*.

——THE AMOUNT OF DNA YOU SHARE WITH . . .——

An identical twin..100 percent

Every other person on Earth...............................99.9 percent

Chimpanzees...98.4 percent

Other animals..90-97 percent

Fruit flies..44 percent

Yeast...26 percent

Weeds..18 percent

DNA is short for deoxyribonucleic acid—a long and complicated molecule found inside every cell of all living things. It is said to be the "blueprint" for life, as every aspect of our physical makeup is determined by it.

——CLANDESTINE GOVERNMENT ORGANIZATIONS——

BOSS   Bureau of State Security: former South African security and intelligence service during apartheid.

CIA   Central Intelligence Agency: U.S. organization responsible for coordinating all intelligence activities.

Gestapo   Secret State Police: secret police force in Nazi Germany, 1936—45.

KGB   Committee of State Security: Russian security police from 1954—91, responsible for counter-intelligence and "crimes against the state" within Russia, and espionage abroad.

MI5   British government agency responsible for intelligence and security on British territory. Its proper name, since 1964, is the Security Service.

MI6   British government agency responsible for intelligence and security overseas. Its proper name, since 1964, is the Secret Intelligence Service (SIS).

Mossad   Supreme Institution for Intelligence and Special Assignments: Israeli secret intelligence service.

——LIGHT, SOUND, AND ELECTRICITY IN ANIMALS——

BIOLUMINESCENCE

This is chemically produced light without heat.

Fireflies and glow-worms use it to send out light signals.

Deep-sea angler fish use it to lure their prey to within gobbling distance.

ECHOLOCATION

Whales and dolphins use a form of sonar that allows them to locate the presence of objects by directing sounds (usually a clicking) toward objects, and interpreting the sound waves that bounce back.

Bats navigate by sending out very high-frequency squeaks, called "ultrasounds," which are reflected off surfaces as echoes.

ELECTRICITY

The electric eel, which is not an eel at all but a fish that is mostly tail, has a body that acts like a battery. The tail end has a positive charge, and the head region a negative charge. When it touches both its head and tail to another beast it sends a strong electric current— 500–650 volts—through the creature, which is enough to stun or kill prey and to ward off predators.

RADAR

The flat disc of feathers that gives certain owls their distinctive face works like a radar dish, catching sounds and directing them to the owl's ears.

THE MEANING OF DREAMS

Dogs	You will make some new friends.
Kittens	A new phase of your life is about to start.
Ears	You should pay close attention to what is being said to you.
Medals	You will be rewarded.
Falling	You are afraid you are going to be in trouble.
Spies	You are feeling guilty.
Guns	You are frightened of something that is going on in your life.
Bird poop on your head	You should spend less time on your appearance.
Butterflies	Someone is going to give you a present.
Balloons	You are especially happy at the moment.
Delicious food	You will soon be rich.
Swords	One of your friends will soon betray you.
Mazes	You are feeling lost.
Wearing slippers to school	You fear you are making a fool of yourself.
Flies	You may soon become unwell.

STRANGE SWALLOWINGS

Strange objects children have swallowed:
coins, safety pins, marbles, rings, batteries, toy parts.

Strange objects adults have swallowed:
false teeth, cutlery, golf balls, toothpicks, screws.

─────THINGS THAT HAVE CLAWS─────

Sloths • Lions • Crowbars • Some bathtubs • Hammers
Tigers • Eagles • Mice • Bears • Squirrels • Vultures • Rats
Koalas • Monkeys • Crabs

─────FIRE TALK─────

Fireball: A ball-shaped bolt of lightning.

Backdraft: The explosion that occurs when air gets into a space where a fire has died out due to lack of oxygen.

Top fire: Fire that spreads from tree-top to tree-top. It can travel at up to 99.4 mph (160 kph).

Crawling fire: Fire that spreads at ground level.

Jumping fire: Fire that is spread by burning leaves and branches.

The Great Fire of London, which started on September 2, 1666, in a bakery in Pudding Lane, raged for four days and destroyed over 13,000 houses. Amazingly, only six people died. The Bakers' Guild was granted formal forgiveness in 1996, 330 years later.

—KING ARTHUR'S KNIGHTS OF THE ROUND TABLE—

Sir Kay • Sir Gareth • Sir Lancelot • Sir Galahad
Sir Bedivere • Sir Gawain • Sir Tristan • Sir Ector • Sir Lionel
Sir Percival • Sir Bors • Sir Tarquin • Sir Mordred

—NAMES CELEBRITIES HAVE GIVEN THEIR CHILDREN—

David and Victoria Beckham.................Brooklyn, Romeo, and Cruz
Gwyneth Paltrow and Chris Martin...Apple
Sting...Fuchsia
David Bowie..Zowie
Frank Zappa..Moon Unit and Dweezil
Will Smith...Willow
Michael Jackson......................Prince Michael I and Prince Michael II
Melanie B ("Scary Spice")...Phoenix Chi
Jason Lee...Pilot Inspektor
Bruce Willis and Demi Moore...................Rumer, Scout, and Tallulah

—————————————CHOCOLATE TIMELINE—————————————

1500–400 BC	The Olmec Indians are the first to grow cocoa trees as a crop.
600 AD	Mayan Indians establish earliest known cocoa plantations in the Yucatán Peninsula, Mexico. They crush the beans into a paste and add spices to make a refreshing and nourishing drink (although it would have been very bitter).
1200s	Aztecs see the tree as a source of strength and wealth, and use the beans as money. They assign their god, Quetzalcóatl, as the tree's guardian.
1500s	European explorers bring the drink back from their travels. Once sweetened, chocolate soon became the fashionable luxury drink.
1847	First ever chocolate bar produced by the British company Fry & Sons.
1861	Richard Cadbury creates the first known heart-shaped chocolate box for Valentine's Day.
1980	An apprentice of the Swiss company Suchard-Tobler tries unsuccessfully to sell secret chocolate recipes to Russia, China, and Saudi Arabia.
Present	The whole world is chocolate crazy! In the United States chocolate consumption is over 11 lb. per person per year—that's about 117 regular-sized chocolate bars. In Western Europe, the average is 18 lb. per person—about 192 bars. The Swiss are the biggest chocolate eaters, eating 22–26 lb. (234–277 bars) per person each year.

————FUNNY FACIAL HAIRSTYLES————

Muttonchops

Friendly
muttonchops

Handlebar

Santa

Chin curtain

Bull

Anchor

Walrus

Freestyle

Goatee

───────THREE CUPS TRICK───────

Place three cups upright on a table.

Turn the middle cup over so that it is upside-down.

Tell your friend that the object of the game is to get all three cups facing downward in just three moves, but you must turn over two cups at a time.

Move 1: turn over the middle and left cup

Move 2: flip the two end cups

Move 3: turn over the two upright cups

You have succeeded. Now turn the middle cup back over LEAVING THE OUTSIDE CUPS FACE DOWN and ask your friend to try.

It is impossible. Your friend has started with the cups in the wrong positions, but probably hasn't noticed!

─ITEMS NOT ALLOWED IN YOUR CARRY-ON LUGGAGE─

Ice picks	Toy guns	Fireworks
Knives	Guns	Aerosols
Meat cleavers	Screwdrivers	Lighters
Swords	Axes	Strike-anywhere matches
Baseball bats	Saws	
Bows and arrows	Drills	Scissors with metal pointed tips
Golf clubs	Cattle prods	
Pool cues	Dynamite	

Lord Oxford was so embarrassed when he farted in front of Queen Elizabeth I that he exiled himself for seven years. When he returned the Queen's first words to him were "My lord, I had forgot the fart."

47

---------------------EXTREME EARTH---------------------

Highest peak	Mount Everest, Himalayas, Nepal-Tibet border, 29,035 ft. (8,850 m).
Lowest water surface	The Dead Sea, Israel-Jordan, 1,349 ft. (411 m) below sea level.
Highest body of water	Lake Titicaca, Bolivia and Peru, 12,500 ft. (3,810 m) above sea level.
Deepest point	Challenger Deep, Mariana Trench, Pacific Ocean, 36,198 ft. (11,033 m) deep.
Tallest waterfall	Angel Falls, Venezuela, dropping 3,212 ft. (979 m).
Longest river	The Nile, Egypt, 4,157 mi. (6,690 km) long.
Largest coral reef	Great Barrier Reef, Australia, 1,257 mi. (2,023 km) long.
Biggest river	The Amazon, South America, 3,978 mi. (6,400 km) long, drains twice as much land as the Nile.

---------------------SKIN DEEP---------------------

Average weight of a person's skin.....................................5.5 lb. (2.5 kg)

Average surface area..16 sq. ft. (1.5 sq. m)

Thinnest..eyelids 0.02 in. (0.5 mm)

Thickest..soles of feet 0.2 in. (5 mm)

Weight shed per night..0.106 oz. (3 g)

Weight shed in a lifetime..40 lb. (18 kg)

MYTHICAL CREATURES

BUNYIP
Monstrous, hippo-like
animal that lives in the
watery Australian outback.

GRIFFIN
Legendary creature with
the head, beak, and wings
of an eagle and the body
and legs of a lion.

TARASQUE
Monster with six
bear-like legs, an ox-like
body covered with a turtle
shell, a scaly tail ending
in a scorpion's sting, a
lion's head, horse's
ears, and the face of
a bitter old man.

KRAKEN
A mile-and-a-half-long,
squid-like sea monster.

NIDHOGG
Serpent-like monster
that eats corpses.

HIPPOCAMPUS
A beast that is half horse
and half fish, with a
serpent's tail.

SPHINX
Monster with the head
of a woman and the body
of a lion.

PHOENIX
Firebird that combusts
and is reborn from
the ashes.

ROC
A huge bird so powerful
it could carry an elephant to
its nest and devour it.

---RIDDLES---

What common English word will describe a person or thing as not being found in any place, and yet with no changes other than adding a space, will correctly describe that person or thing as being actually present at this very moment?
(Nowhere — Now here)

Pete likes beets but not spinach. He likes apples but not pears. He likes jeeps but not vans. He likes Sally but not Sarah. Who will he like — Jimmy or Joe?
(Jimmy — double letters)

Anna has the same number of brothers as she has sisters, but her brother Nat has twice as many sisters as he has brothers. How many boys and how many girls are there in the family?
(4 girls, 3 boys)

Two dogs are sitting on a porch — a fat dog and a thin dog. The thin dog is the son of the fat dog, but the fat dog is not the father of the thin dog. How can this be?
(The fat dog is the thin dog's mother.)

---MICRO OR NANO?---

MICROMETER (μm)
one millionth of a meter ($1/1{,}000{,}000$ m or about $1/25{,}000$ in.)

A human hair is 100 μm thick.

A bacterium is 1 μm wide.

NANOMETER (nm)
one-thousand-millionth of a meter ($1/1{,}000{,}000{,}000$ m or about $1/25{,}000{,}000$ in.)

A common-cold virus is 100 nm wide
(i.e. one-tenth the size of a bacterium).

An atom is $1/10$ nm across.

REAL-LIFE PIRATES

Grace O'Malley (Gráinne ni Mháille), "Pirate Queen of
Connacht" 1530–1603

Sir Henry Morgan 1635–1688

William Kidd, "Captain Kidd" 1645–1701

William Dampier (famed as an explorer) 1652–1715

Samuel Bellamy, "Black Bellamy" d. 1717

Jack Rackham, "Calico Jack" d. 1720

Edward Teach, "Blackbeard" 1680–1718

Anne Bonney 1697/8–1720

Mary Read d. 1721

Jean Laffite *c.* 1780–*c.* 1826

WHAT DO TOOTHLESS ANIMALS EAT?

Blue whale...Krill (tiny shrimp-like creatures)

Tortoise..Tears off leaves with its horny beak

Anteater...Scoops up ants and other insects
with its long tongue

Pangolin.....................................Eats termites, uses stones and sand to
help break down food

I INVENTED IT. NO, I INVENTED IT

Whom shall we credit with the following inventions?

THE TELEPHONE
The German physicist Johann Philipp Reis, who in 1861
produced a device called the Telephon, which transmitted
electrical tones through wires, OR
Scottish-Canadian-American Alexander Graham Bell, in 1876,
OR the American Elisha Gray, who may have just beaten Bell
to the mailbox?

THE ZIPPER
Elias Howe in 1851, with his Automatic Continuous
Clothing Closure, OR
Whitcomb Judson, with his Clasp Locker in 1893, OR
Swedish-born Canadian Gideon Sundback, with his Separable
Fastener in 1917?

THE LIGHT BULB
Heinrich Göbel in 1854—he later won a court case
against Thomas Edison, OR
Joseph Wilson Swan in Britain in 1878, OR
Thomas Edison in 1879?

WHAT YELLOW MEANS

Warning • Warmth • Happiness • Glory • Mourning • Activity
Creativity • Illness • Jealousy • Cowardice • Courage

————————HOW TO WRITE A HAIKU————————

A haiku (from the Japanese *haikai no ku*, meaning "light verse") is a classical three-line Japanese verse form that follows the pattern below. Traditionally, a haiku is about nature, but you can write yours about whatever you like.

LINE	SYLLABLES	SUGGESTED CONTENT
1	5	The subject of the haiku
2	7	What the subject does
3	5	A summarizing punchline

Example One:
Sunlight on water
Dapples the riverbed where
Hides the spotted trout.

Example Two:
Black-and-white mayhem
Bounces among the branches,
Hungry for baubles.

————————EXCUSE ME————————

Chinese (Mandarin)..............................."Dui bu qui"

Croatian.."Oprostite"

Dutch..."Pardon"

French..."Pardonnez-moi"

German.."Entschuldigung"

Greek..."Suggnome"

Iranian (Persian/Farsi)......................"Bebakhshid"

Italian..."Scusi"

Japanese.."Sumimasen"

Polish......................................."Przepraszam"

Russian and Serbian................................"Izvinite"

Spanish.."Perdón"

Swedish.."Ursäkta"

Yiddish..."Antshuldik(t)"

INCREDIBLE INSECTS

Smallest.................................Fairyfly wasp, wingspan 0.008 in. (0.2 mm)

Largest................White Birdwing butterfly, wingspan 12 in. (30.5 mm)

Longest.............................Giant stick insect, total length 20 in. (50 cm)

Heaviest..Goliath beetle, weight 3.5 oz. (100 gm)

Loudest.............................Cicada, can be heard from 0.25 mi. (400 m)

Most beautiful..Madagascan sunset moth

Best jumper.................Flea, can jump 150 times its own body length

Fastest flyer...Dragonfly, 35 mph (56 kph)

Longest living............................Queen of termites, lives 50−100 years

Most dangerous.............Australian bulldog ant, sting can kill humans

Most social............Ants, work together in highly organized colonies

Most annoying...Tiny biting midge

The oldest playable musical instrument is a flute that was discovered in an ancient burial site in China. It is over 9,000 years old and is carved from a bird's wing bone. It can still be played, making a high reedy sound, not unlike a penny whistle.

YY U R YY U B I C U R YY 4 ME

Too wise you are, too wise you be,
I see you are too wise for me.

—————FAMOUS NOBEL PRIZE WINNERS—————

Marie Curie	Physics (research into radioactivity), 1903, and Chemistry (discovery of radium and polonium), 1911
Theodore Roosevelt	Peace (collaboration on various peace treaties), 1906
Rudyard Kipling	Literature (novels, poems, and short stories including *The Jungle Book*), 1907
Albert Einstein	Physics (discovery of the law of the photoelectric effect), 1921
T. S. Eliot	Literature (outstanding contribution to poetry), 1948
John Steinbeck	Literature (novels including *The Grapes of Wrath* and *Of Mice and Men*), 1962
Francis Harry Compton Crick and James Dewey Watson	Medicine (discovery of the structure of DNA), 1962
Martin Luther King, Jr.	Peace (leader of the "Southern Christian Leadership Conference"), 1964
Mother Teresa	Peace (leader of "Missionaries of Charity"), 1979
Nelson Mandela	Peace (peaceful termination of the apartheid regime in South Africa), 1993

————REAL ALTERNATIVES TO TOILET PAPER————

Water • Hands • Newspapers or magazines
Leaves • Stones • Shells • Feathers • Corn cobs • Rope
Sticks • Sand • Rags • Wet sponge • Money

HOW MANY MAGPIES?

One for sorrow,

Two for joy,

Three for a girl,

Four for a boy,

Five for silver,

Six for gold,

Seven for a secret never to be told.

MESSAGE NOT ALWAYS FULLY UNDERSTOOD

Your nerves send messages to the brain, but their messages are not always that accurate. Try this experiment with a friend.

1. Have one arm bare to the elbow. Shut your eyes and keep them shut.

2. Ask your friend to tap the inside of your forearm gently with a fingertip. He or she should start at the wrist, then progress slowly up toward your elbow.

3. When you think your friend has reached the crease on the inside of your elbow, tell your friend to stop, and open your eyes.

4. Has your friend's finger reached the inside of your elbow, or has your brain misunderstood the message?

> Farts are made up of five different gases, mainly nitrogen. The smell comes from substances in your poop called skatole and indole (ironically both are used in the manufacture of perfumes).

—————————SIEGE ENGINES—————————

BALLISTA

A machine like a giant crossbow that used wound-up ropes to fire a projectile (usually a rock) straight and low.

SPRING ENGINE

Similar to a ballista, but used spring arms of metal or horn to fire a heavy iron dart, like a giant crossbow bolt.

TREBUCHET

Used a counterweight at the end of a long pivoted arm to fling very large (up to half a ton) boulders and other projectiles, including balls of flaming pitch and the heads of captured enemies, high in the air for considerable distances.

TRACTION CATAPULT

Worked like a trebuchet, but used human power (usually several soldiers heaving together), instead of a counterweight, to pull down one end of a long pivoted arm to release the projectile in a sling at the other end.

ONAGER

Meaning "wild donkey," probably because it "kicked" like one. This was like a cross between a ballista and a trebuchet, and used wound-up ropes to propel a catapult arm, hurling a projectile from a cup at the long end of the arm.

STRANGE REMEDIES

EYE DISEASES
Bathe eyes with rainwater collected before dawn in June • Apply a mixture of tortoise brain and honey Rub with the tail of a black cat • Dab with a few drops of urine

TOOTHACHE
Press a new nail into the gum and aching tooth until it bleeds, then hammer the nail into a tree • Burn one ear with a hot poker • Tie a dead mole around your neck

DIARRHEA
Eat gruel • Green onions Oil • Honey • Wax and water • Coca leaves

COMMON COLD
Put mustard and onions up your nose • Tie a sweaty sock around your neck

WARTS
Dab with dog's pee Spread pig's blood on them Daub with mashed-up slugs Stroke with the tail of a tortoiseshell cat in the month of May • Dribble over the warts first thing in the morning

HEADACHE
Drill a hole in your skull Rub cow dung on the temples • Lean head against a tree while someone drives a nail into the opposite side of the trunk • Tie the head of a buzzard round your neck • Sleep with a pair of "pain-cutting" scissors under the pillow

GOITER AND TUMORS
Touch with a hanged man's hand

THINGS THAT HARM THE PLANET

Burning fossil fuels

Cars and airplanes

Wasting things

Leaving on the TV/lights/heating/electricity

Using detergents and bleach

Leaving faucets on

Dumping trash/littering

HOW TO FLY A HELICOPTER

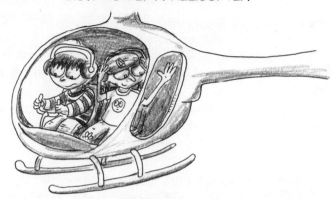

A helicopter can move up and down, forward and backward, and sideways. It can also rotate 360 degrees, stop in midair and hover . . . and while hovering it can spin round. As a helicopter pilot you must be at your most alert to be able to operate and control the movement of the craft.

1. In one hand you have the collective pitch stick. This adjusts the main rotors so that the chopper can go up and down. It also controls the engine speed.

2. In the other hand you have the cyclic pitch. This control makes the main rotor tilt so that it can pull the helicopter backward, forward, or sideways.

3. Your feet rest on pedals that control the tail rotor, which allows the helicopter to turn to face any direction.

To perfect your flight and avoid embarrassing wild spins, dipping this way and that, and jerky rises and drops in the air, you have to make sure that your hands and feet work together. A skillful pilot can keep the craft hovering in a high wind and show off by pirouetting down to a landing space.

THINGS THAT SHRINK

Icebergs • Old people

SPORTING LOSERS

BOXING
Daniel Caruso was so enthusiastic while warming up for the Golden Gloves Championships in 1992 that he punched himself in the face and broke his nose. Doctors decided he was unfit to fight.

MARATHON RUNNING
Leda Diaz de Cano was so far behind the other competitors in the 1984 Olympics that officials had to persuade her to give up so they could reopen the streets to traffic.

MOTORCYCLING
While waving to the crowd after finishing fourth in the 500cc U.S. Motorcycle Championship in 1989, Kevin Magee fell off his bike and broke his leg.

RUGBY
A team from Doncaster, UK, lost 40 games in a row. On one occasion the players failed to recognize their own strip because they were covered in mud, and began to tackle their own side.

SOCCER
Rio Ferdinand, the world's most expensive defender, strained a tendon behind his knee not while he was in training, but by putting his foot up on the coffee table while watching television.

THE WORST PLACE TO . . .

Eat a hamburger..On a roller coaster

Fall over..In a stinging-nettle patch

Fart..In the principal's office

Cut yourself....................................In a river full of piranhas

Skateboard..On gravel

Have a giggling fit....................................In assembly

Bang yourself..On your funny bone

Be sick...In a tent

————THE RHYMING WEATHER FORECAST————

Red sky at morning, sailors take warning.
Red sky at night, sailors' delight.

When the dew is on the grass, rain will never come to pass.

Ring around the moon, rain by noon.
Ring around the sun, rain before night is done.

Rain before seven, fine before eleven.

A cow with its tail to the west makes the weather best,
A cow with its tail to the east makes the weather least.

If the oak is out before the ash then we are in for a splash.
But if the ash is out before the oak we are in for a soak.

The rain, it raineth on the just
And also on the unjust fella:
But chiefly on the just, because
The unjust steals the just's umbrella.

THINGS WE USE TREES FOR

Oxygen
Shade
Fuel
Buildings
Furniture
Musical instruments
Reducing noise pollution
Lowering air temperature
Vital drugs
Paper
Rubber
Building blocks
Homes for birds
Tree houses

SHAKESPEAREAN INSULTS

"Your bum is the greatest thing about you."
(*Measure for Measure*)

"Pray you, stand farther away from me."
(*Antony and Cleopatra*)

"Thou art a boil, a plague-sore, an embossed carbuncle."
(*King Lear*)

"You Banbury cheese!"
(*The Merry Wives of Windsor*)

"Thy food is such as hath been belched on by infected lungs."
(*Pericles, Prince of Tyre*)

"Were I like thee, I'd throw away myself."
(*Timon of Athens*)

ABBREVIATIONS

AKA..Also Known As
ASAP...As Soon As Possible
DVD...Digital Versatile Disc
ETA..Estimated Time of Arrival
ISP...Internet Service Provider
FYI..For Your Information
BTW...By The Way
RSVP...........................Répondez S'il Vous Plaît (please reply)
TWAIN..................Technology Without Any Interesting Name
MYOB...Mind Your Own Business
AWOL.......................................Absent Without Leave
BYO...Bring Your Own
TBC...To Be Confirmed
SWAT.................................Special Weapons and Tactics
SCUBA....Self-Contained Underwater Breathing Apparatus

FAMOUS
REAL-LIFE DOGS

Pickles, the dog who found the stolen Soccer World Cup in 1966.

Strelka and Belka, who returned safely to Earth after a day in space in 1960.

Barry, a St. Bernard who rescued over 40 people stranded in the Alps.

Rico, a Border collie who understands over 200 words.

FAMOUS
REAL-LIFE CATS

Sugar, the cat who walked some 1,500 miles across the United States to rejoin her owners, who had given her away when they moved.

Scarlett, who rescued her five kittens from a burning building in New York in 1996.

Solomon, the white chinchilla longhair who played Blofeld's cat in the James Bond films.

FORTUNE TELLER

To make a fortune teller all you need is a square piece of paper and some colored pens.

1. Fold the square in half from one corner to the other.

2. Fold it again, to form a smaller triangle. Then unfold the sheet and lay it flat.

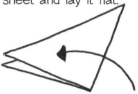

3. Fold each corner of the square into the middle, so the corners all meet at the center.

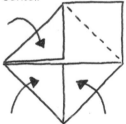

4. Turn the fortune teller over, and repeat step 3, folding the new corners into the middle.

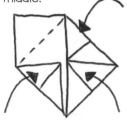

5. Turn the sheet over so that you can see four squares, then fold in half with the squares on the outside.

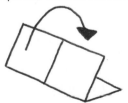

6. Finally, keeping the squares on the outside, fold in half the other way.

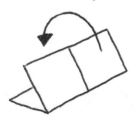

7. Use colored pens to put a different colored blob on each of the four outer squares.

8. Write a different number on each of the eight inner triangles.

9. Lift up each of the numbered triangles and write a fortune, such as "You will be rich and famous" or "You will live in another country" underneath.

10. Slide the thumb and forefinger of both your hands under the flaps of your fortune teller.

11. Ask a friend to choose one of the colors on the flaps of your fortune teller. Spell out the color, opening and closing the fortune teller for each letter. On the last letter, hold the fortune teller open and ask your friend to choose one of the four numbers that show inside.

12. Count out that number, opening and closing the fortune teller, then ask your friend to choose another number and count it out the same way.

13. Ask your friend to pick a final number. Open up the flap beneath that number and read your friend's fortune.

You can use fortune tellers for lots of other things by changing what you write under the number flaps. Instead of writing fortunes you could try dares, questions, insults, the names of your friends' true loves, or anything else you can think of.

——————VITAMIN DEFICIENCIES——————

VITAMIN AND WHERE TO FIND IT	SYMPTOMS OF DEFICIENCY
Vitamin A (carrots, cabbage)	Scaly skin, poor growth
Vitamin B1 (thiamine) (pork, split peas)	Beriberi: loss of appetite, tiredness, aching joints, numbness in hands and feet, heart problems
Vitamin B2 (riboflavin) (cereal, milk)	Poor digestion, eye disorders, dry and flaky skin, sore red tongue
Vitamin B3 (niacin) (chicken, tuna)	Pellagra: weakness, skin inflammation, diarrhea, weight loss, depression, confusion, memory loss
Vitamin B6 (pyridoxine) (beans, fish)	Depression, nausea, weakness, greasy and flaky skin
Vitamin B7 or H (biotin) (eggs, spinach)	Heart abnormalities, appetite loss, fatigue, depression, dry skin
Vitamin B12 (beef, shellfish)	Anemia, fatigue, nerve damage, smooth tongue, very sensitive skin
Vitamin C (oranges, strawberries)	Scurvy: tiredness, aching, sores that won't heal, swollen gums, loss of teeth
Vitamin D (salmon, eggs)	Rickets: deformed skull, curved spine, bowed legs, knobby growths on ends of bones
Vitamin E (almonds, peanuts)	Nervous-system problems
Vitamin K (broccoli, cheese)	Thin blood, danger of bleeding to death

> Ask a friend to think of a word that rhymes with orange, purple, or silver.

—TOP FIVE ALL-TIME WORLDWIDE BOX-OFFICE HITS—

ONE
Titanic (1997)

TWO
*The Lord of the Rings:
The Return of the King* (2003)

THREE
*Harry Potter and the
Sorcerer's Stone* (2001)

FOUR
*Star Wars Episode I:
The Phantom Menace* (1999)

FIVE
*The Lord of the Rings:
The Two Towers* (2002)

THE CHINESE CALENDAR

1995	Pig
1996	Rat
1997	Cow
1998	Tiger
1999	Rabbit
2000	Dragon
2001	Snake
2002	Horse
2003	Goat
2004	Monkey
2005	Rooster
2006	Dog

And then back to pig—it is a 12-year cycle.

PHRENOLOGY

According to phrenology, all the many aspects of a person's character can be seen in "bumps" on the surface of the brain. As the personality developed so would the bumps—those corresponding to much-used characteristics growing and those corresponding to little-used characteristics shrinking. These bumps could change with character over time. The diagram below shows which bumps relate to which characteristics.

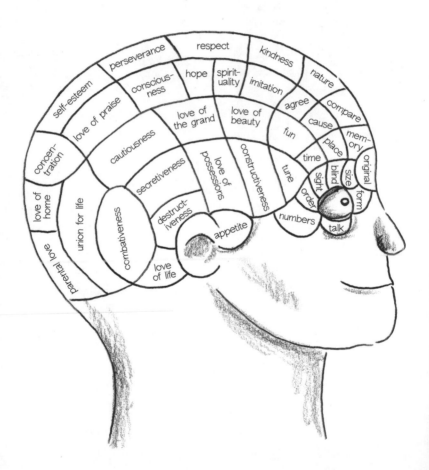

————CAUSES OF CROP CIRCLES: THEORIES————

Landscape artists • Evil entities • Aliens

Freak whirlwinds • Unknown natural energies • Hoaxers

Intelligent balls of white light

————————BODY APPENDAGES————————

CLAY LIP PLATES
(Mursi people, Omo Valley, Ethiopia)
When a Mursi girl reaches the age of 15 or 16, her bottom lip
is pierced and a clay lip plate is inserted. As the lip stretches,
larger and larger plates are inserted. It is thought that the
larger the lip plate, the greater the number of cattle required
in exchange for her hand in marriage.

BRASS NECK RINGS
(Padaung tribe, Burma)
As young girls, women from the Padaung tribe are given brass
rings to wear around their necks. As they grow up, more and
more rings are added and this gives them the appearance of
having extraordinarily long necks. In fact, the rings do not
stretch the neck, but rather the weight of them pushes down
on the collarbone and shoulders.

EARLOBE PIERCINGS
(global)
In Western culture it is common for men and women to pierce
their ears. Sometimes, by gradually increasing the size of the
part of the ring that goes through the lobe, people increase
the size of the holes to accommodate large earplugs.

————ANIMALS THAT CAN CHANGE COLOR————

Chameleon • Flounder • Octopus • Cuttlefish

Golden tortoise beetle • Bark spider

------------------SPACE FIRSTS------------------

FIRST SATELLITE
Soviet Russia's *Sputnik 1*,
launched into orbit around
Earth on October 4, 1957.

FIRST ANIMAL IN SPACE
Laika, a dog, on board
Soviet Russia's *Sputnik 2* on
November 3, 1957.

FIRST MAN IN SPACE
Soviet Russian cosmonaut
Yuri Gagarin aboard *Vostok 1*
on April 12, 1961.

FIRST WOMAN IN SPACE
Soviet Russian cosmonaut
Valentina Tereshkova, who
piloted *Vostok 6* in orbit
around Earth for four days
in 1963.

FIRST SPACE WALK
Soviet Russian Aleksei A.
Leonov, on March 18, 1965,
left the *Voskhod 2*
spacecraft and floated
tethered in space for
12 minutes.

FIRST SPACE STATION
Soviet Russia's *Salyut 1*,
launched in April 1971.

FIRST SPACE SHUTTLE
America's *Columbia*, launched
on April 12, 1981.

FIRST MOON LANDING
Soviet Russia's *Luna 9*,
launched January 31, 1966.

FIRST MOON WALK
American astronaut
Neil Armstrong, commander
of the *Apollo 11* lunar
mission, walked on the
Moon on July 20, 1969.

FIRST WORDS SPOKEN
ON THE MOON
"OK, Houston, I'm on the
porch . . . I'm at the foot
of the ladder. The LEM
footpads are on the, uh,
depressed in the surface
about one or two inches.
Going to step off the
LEM now. That's one
small step for [a] man,
one giant leap for
mankind." Neil Armstrong on
July 20, 1969.

ARE YOU IN PROPORTION?

Fingertip to wrist = Hairline to chin

Big toe to heel = Elbow to wrist

Outstretched fingertip to outstretched fingertip = Head to toe

Knee to ankle = Elbow to fingertip

ONOMATOPOEIC WORDS

(Words that sound like what they refer to.)

SPLASH	SQUEAK	HUSH	GRUNT
WHINE	CRACKLE	CHIME	HISS
THUD	BABBLE	BOOM	POP
CLANG	TINKLE	PING-PONG	HOOT
PURR	MOAN	WHIRR	GONG

THE GREAT PYRAMID OF KHUFU (OR CHEOPS) AT GIZA

Built: 2589−2566 BC

Purpose: Pharaoh Khufu's burial chamber

Time to build: 20 years

Number of laborers: 20,000−30,000

Machinery used: elementary "cranes," manpower, scaffolding, ropes of papyrus twine, ramps of stone, wood, and mud

Weight: 6 million tons

Number of "bricks" (granite and limestone blocks): 2,300,000

Height on completion: 481 ft. (146.5 m)

Height now: 449 ft. (137 m)

Amazing fact: It was the tallest building in the world until the early 20th century—some 45 centuries!

THE ENIGMA MACHINE

The Enigma machine was a portable electrical and mechanical device for encoding and decoding messages. Invented by a German in 1918, it was housed in a wooden case and resembled an old-fashioned typewriter keyboard, with a set of removable and interchangeable wheels (rotors) toward the back, and letter keys at the front.

By the Second World War, the machine had been adopted by the German armed forces and modified to suit their needs, then produced in large quantities. The Germans believed unquestioningly that the Allies would never be able to break the machine's codes as there were so many thousands of possibilities. There was one weak spot, though: the day's settings for a machine had to be sent between encoder and decoder, and these settings were often captured by the Allies. One of the machines was intercepted in Poland and smuggled to Britain. Then, with the help of some Polish mathematicians, cryptologists based in Buckinghamshire, UK, succeeded in breaking the codes of a large number of intercepted Nazi messages, and gained vital military intelligence from them.

WHAT RED MEANS

Stop • Danger • Emergency • Love • Passion
Hatred • Anger • Power • Energy • Importance • Luck
Success • Happiness • Prosperity

WHO IS THAT CELEBRITY?

Dido..................................Florian Cloud de Bounevialle Armstrong

Elton John..................Elton Hercules John Reginald Kenneth Dwight

Eminem..Marshall Bruce Mathers

Jennifer Aniston...............................Jennifer Linn Anastassakis

Macy Gray...Natalie Renee McIntyre

Marilyn Manson...Brian Warner

Nicolas Cage...Nicholas Kim Coppola

Pink...Alecia Moore

Puff Daddy...Sean John Combs

Ringo Starr...Richard Starkey

> The first number (written
> out) to have the letter "a" in
> it is "one hundred and one."

SURVIVORS OF ASSASSINATION ATTEMPTS

Elizabeth I, Queen of England (1570)

Napoleon I, Emperor of France (1809)

Theodore Roosevelt, President of the United States (1912)

Adolf Hitler, German dictator (1944)

Andy Warhol, American artist (1968)

Bob Marley, Jamaican reggae singer (1976)

Pope John Paul II (1981 and 1995)

Margaret Thatcher, British Prime Minister (1984)

Jacques Chirac, President of France (2002)

Romero Prodi, Italian Prime Minister (2003)

———— AN ALCHEMIST'S RECIPE FOR GOLD————

PART 1

Agents

1 lb. vitriol, 1 lb. sal ammoniac, 1 lb. arinat, 1 lb. sal nitrate,
1 lb. sal gemmae, 1 lb. alumen crudum, ground antimony
ore (antimonium)

Method

Mix all the agents except the antimonium thoroughly.
Place in a conical flask over a Bunsen burner, and distill to
form a liquid. Dissolve the antimonium in this liquid and
leave until solid deposits are formed. Remove these solids
and wash them.

PART 2

Agents

Distilled vinegar

Method

Put the solids from part 1 in a vial and pour in the distilled
vinegar. Place the vial in a pan of hot water, and leave
for 40 days. You will now have a red liquid. Pour this liquid
into a flask and mix with some more distilled vinegar. Distill
the solution to create a dry powder.

PART 3

Agents

Distilled water, spirit wine

Method

Wash the powder from part 2 with the distilled water, and
leave to dry. The antimonium will now be bright red in
color. Place the antimonium in vial, add the spirit wine,
and place in a pan of warm water for four days.

Repeat this process of distillation and refinement
until you have created the purest gold.

─────── "FACTS" THAT ARE NOT TRUE ───────

Chewing gum takes seven years to pass through the human
digestive system, if it doesn't kill you first.

The word *nylon* is from <u>N</u>ew <u>Y</u>ork and <u>Lon</u>don.

The bra was invented by Otto Titzling.

There are alligators living in New York City's sewers.

The French queen Marie Antoinette said "Let them eat cake"
when she heard that the country's poor had no bread.

No two snowflakes are alike.

Elephants are afraid of mice.

─────── ANIMALS THAT METAMORPHOSE ───────

frogspawn	tadpole	froglet	frog
egg	caterpillar	chrysalis	butterfly
egg	caterpillar	cocoon	moth
egg	maggot	pupa	fly
egg	grub	pupa	beetle
egg	larva	nymph	dragonfly

75

────── POSSIBLE OR IMPOSSIBLE?──────

──WHAT DO YOU GET WHEN YOU CROSS . . .──

A vampire and a snowman?..Frostbite

A centipede and a parrot?..A walkie-talkie

A karate expert and a pig?..A pork chop

A fish and two elephants?..Swimming trunks

A cat and a duck?..A duck-filled fatty puss

A beetle and a rabbit?..Bugs Bunny

Rudolph and a weatherman?..Rain, dear

A frog and a parking enforcer?..Toad away

A computer and a potato?..Microchips

A flea and some moon rock?..A lunar-tick

GREAT WARRIORS

HANNIBAL
247–182 BC—Carthaginian general who marched a huge army (including 40 elephants) across the Alps from Spain to attack Rome. Many years later he killed himself rather than surrender to the Romans.

TAMERLANE
1336–1405—Mongol emperor who was partially paralyzed on his left side. He conquered a huge area stretching from the Mediterranean to western India and all the way up to Russia. He was extremely cruel to his enemies and built pyramids of skulls every time he destroyed a city.

ALEXANDER THE GREAT
356–323 BC—King of Macedonia. He was taught by the philosopher Aristotle and could tame wild horses. At 20, he became king and managed to crush a Greek rebellion and conquer Persia, Egypt, and part of India, all before he died at the age of 33.

ATTILA THE HUN
406–453 BC—Killed his brother to become king and is said to have eaten two of his children. Formed a huge army and destroyed many cities in the Roman Empire. He eventually died of a nosebleed after getting very drunk on his wedding night.

HOW FAST IS THE WORLD SPINNING?

The Earth spins on an axis that runs from the North Pole to the South Pole. This means that the farther away you get from the poles, the faster the earth spins.

North and South Pole	0 mph (0 kph)
Iceland	345 mph (700 kph)
United Kingdom	615 mph (990 kph)
Spain	746 mph (1,200 kph)
Central USA	746 mph (1,200 kph)
Australia	870 mph (1,400 kph)
Kenya (equator)	994 mph (1,600 kph)

SILLY SIGNS

In a church: "A bean supper will be held on Tuesday evening in the church hall. Music will follow."

In a safari park: "Elephants please stay in your car."

At a post office: "This door is not to be used as an exit or an entrance."

In a park: "No cycling dogs on leashes."

On a roadside: "Animals drive very slowly."

At a zoo: "Those who throw objects at the crocodiles will be asked to retrieve them."

At an optician's: "If you don't see what you're looking for, you've come to the right place."

THE PHONETIC ALPHABET

A	Alpha	H	Hotel	O	Oscar	V	Victor
B	Bravo	I	India	P	Papa	W	Whisky
C	Charlie	J	Juliet	Q	Quebec	X	X-ray
D	Delta	K	Kilo	R	Romeo	Y	Yankee
E	Echo	L	Lima	S	Sierra	Z	Zulu
F	Foxtrot	M	Mike	T	Tango		
G	Golf	N	November	U	Uniform		

CRIMINAL MASTERMINDS?

Two car-radio thieves in Austria were busted when police followed footprints they had left in the snow from car to car, and then to their apartment.

Romanian police were questioning a pair of women about a cell phone reported stolen. When one of the officers dialed the number of the stolen phone, a ringing was heard—from one of the suspects' underpants.

In China, a young burglar broke into an office and filled up his bag with cash and valuables. Then he looked in the fridge and ate the cakes and drank the milk he found there. Feeling tired, he lay down for a bit. Members of staff arriving in the morning found him still there, fast asleep.

In Wales, an armed bank robber waited patiently while the cashier carefully counted and then recounted the money he was to hand over. By the time he had finished counting, very slowly, the police had arrived.

An armed bank robber in Iowa got his cash and jumped into his getaway car. The vehicle had a personalized license plate that carried the thief's last name.

In the United States, a police officer tried calling the car phone of a lady whose vehicle had been stolen. When the car thief answered, the officer pretended that he had seen a notice advertising the car for sale and was interested in buying it. Suspecting nothing, the thief made an appointment to meet the officer.

In the United States, a burglar broke into a home and made away with various electronic articles, including a digital camera. Stupidly, he took a photo of himself that he forgot to delete before taking it to a pawnshop.

In Japan, an armed burglar broke into what he thought were the offices of Japan Railways and loudly demanded money— to find himself surrounded by police officers. He'd broken into a police dormitory.

──────SOMETHING FISHY──────

HAGFISH
A primitive marine fish with a slimy, eel-like body and no proper jaw. It has a slit-like mouth, and feeds off dead or dying fish.

SEA HORSE
A small marine fish with a tube-like snout, segmented bony armor, and a curled tail. It swims upright in the water.

COELACANTH
Last surviving relative of a prehistoric group of fishes. It was thought to be long extinct until 1938, when one was captured alive.

PIPEFISH
A long, thin tubular fish resembling a straightened-out seahorse (to which it's related).

LUNGFISH
Has two primitive lungs, allowing it to breathe air so that it can survive out of water and live in mud for long periods during droughts.

PUFFER FISH
Various species of globe-shaped fish with spiny skins; when alarmed or threatened, they can inflate themselves with air or water like a balloon. Can be poisonous.

──────I FEEL THE NEED, THE NEED FOR SPEED──────

Speed of light....................................671,000,000 mph (1,080,000,000 kph)

Speed of sound..758 mph (1,220 kph)

Fastest passenger plane...............Concorde, 1,450 mph (2,333 kph)

Land speed record..763 mph (1,228 kph)

Fastest passenger train...........France's TGV, 320.2 mph (515.3 kph)

Fastest animal...........................Peregrine falcon, 200 mph (321.9 kph)

Fastest land animal......................................Cheetah, 62.1 mph (100 kph)

Fastest two-legged animal.........................Ostrich, 43.5 mph (70 kph)

Fastest human...................................Asafa Powell, 22.9 mph (36.8 kph)

Fastest snail..0.03 mph (0.048 kph)

—HOW TO TURN YOUR WATCH INTO A COMPASS—

You will need: a wristwatch with hands, set to the correct local time. You need to be able to see the sun (even if it's shining through clouds). Most important of all, you also need to know that the sun rises in the east and sets in the west; and that at 12 noon in the northern hemisphere it is due south (in the southern hemisphere it's due north).

With the watch horizontal, aim the hour hand at the sun. Then exactly divide the angle between the position of the hour hand and the 12 on the watch face—the line that follows that angle is the north-south line. But which end of the line is north? If it's morning, north will be on the right side of the watch face (12-1-2-3-4-5-6). If it's afternoon, north will be on the left side (6-7-8-9-10-11-12).

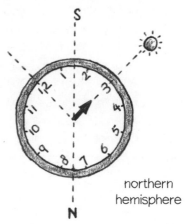

northern hemisphere

If you have a digital watch, draw a watch face on a piece of paper, mark the 12, and then draw in the hour hand in the position for the time shown on your digital. Next, aim the hour hand in the drawing at the sun and follow the procedure as for a watch with hands (technically termed an analog watch).

If you are in the southern hemisphere, aim the 12 on the watch face at the sun and find the north-south line by bisecting the angle between the hour hand and 12. In the morning north will be on the left side of the watch face; in the afternoon north will be on the right side.

The average four-year-old asks over 400 questions a day.

THE ORIGINS OF TEXT MESSAGING

1844   First telegraph message: "What hath God wrought." (Samuel Morse)

1861   First message on a "Telephon": "A horse does not eat a cucumber salad." (Johann Philipp Reis)

1876   First words transmitted by telephone: "Mr. Watson, come here; I want you." (Alexander Graham Bell)

1901   First transatlantic radio message: "dot-dot-dot," meaning "s" in Morse code. (Guglielmo Marconi)

1924   First facsimile (fax) message transmitted across Atlantic, from New York to Sweden.

1949   First message sent by telephone pager. (Al Gross)

1973   First call on a cell phone (by the inventor Martin Cooper to his main rival).

1992   First text message sent.

EMOTICONS

:-)	I'm happy
:-(	I'm sad
;-)	I'm winking
:-D	I'm laughing
:'-(	I'm crying
:'-D	I'm crying with laughter
:-|	I'm bored
:-X	kiss
:-0	oops!
:=(	Pee-yew!
8-p	Yuck!
^^^	Giggles
:-#	I got braces

REAL NEWSPAPER HEADLINES

Iraqi Head Seeks Arms

Drunk Gets Nine Months in Violin Case

British Left Waffles on Falkland Islands

Two Sisters Reunited after 18 Years in Checkout

War Dims Hope for Peace

Typhoon Rips Through Cemetery: Hundreds Dead

Chef Throws His Heart into Helping Feed Needy

Air Head Fired

Kids Make Nutritious Snacks

Enraged Cow Injures Farmer with Axe

—CARTOON CATS—	—CARTOON DOGS—
Felix	Goofy
Tom	Pluto
Top Cat	Snoopy
Sylvester	Santa's Little Helper
Garfield	Scooby Doo

——————WHO'S THE TALLEST?——————

————REDS, BLUES, AND GREENS————

Brick	Aquamarine	Apple
Burgundy	Azure	Avocado
Carmine	Cerulean	Beryl
Claret	Cobalt	Chartreuse
Crimson	Cornflower	Emerald
Maroon	Cyan	Fir
Rose madder	Indigo	Leaf
Rouge	Navy	Lime
Ruby	Prussian	Moss
Russet	Robin's egg	Olive
Rust	Royal	Pine
Scarlet	Sapphire	Sage
Vermilion	Ultramarine	Sea
	Periwinkle	

WAYS TO CHOOSE WHO IS "IT"

Everyone makes a fist with both hands. You then go around the group touching one fist for each of the words of one of the rhymes below. The fist that the last word lands on is out. The rhyme is repeated until just one fist is left, and that person is "it."

"Ip dip sky blue who's it not you."

"One potato, two potato, three potato, four, five potato, six potato, seven potato, more—that means you are not it."

"Ippy dippy dation my operation how many people at the station"—at this point the person whose fist you're on gives a number, e.g. 3, that you then count out—"one, two, three."

"Ibble obble black bobble ibble obble out."

"Dip dip dip, my blue ship, sails on the water,
like a cup and saucer—O-U-T spells out."

WHAT DOES YOUR HANDWRITING SAY ABOUT YOU?

Large letters.............Flamboyant and outgoing, a bit of a show-off

Small letters.........................Timid and shy with a good eye for detail

Right-sloping letters..........................Open and honest, likes attention

Left-sloping letters...Shy and reserved

Upright letters.............................Fair and always willing to listen

Lines slant upward..Positive, optimistic

Lines slant downward.........A bit moody, could do with cheering up

Lines slant up and down...................................Unpredictable, indecisive

Rounded letters............................Logical and usually gets things right

Spiky letters...Quick-thinking and perceptive

All capital letters..Trying to hide something

Unusual dots...Artistic and creative

Regular and neat.................Reliable, organized, and good in a crisis

Great Britain was the first country to issue postage stamps, which is why theirs are the only stamps in the world not to bear the name of the country of origin. The first stamp was issued on May 1, 1840, and became known as the Penny Black.

---THINGS THAT ARE FUN TO SAY---

"Eenie-meanie-macka-racka-rare-rar-domi-nacka-chicker-pocker-lolly-popper-om-pom-push"

"Glockenspiel"

"Super-cali-fragi-listic-expi-ali-docious"

"In a tiny house, by a tiny stream, sat a lovely lass, who had a lovely dream, and the dream came true, quite unexpectedly, in a gilly gilly hoser-neffer-kaba-neller-bogen by the sea."

"Antidisestablishmentarianism"

"Tell me no secrets I'll tell you no lies, I saw a policeman zipping his flies are a nuisance bees are worse, and that is the end of my silly little verse."

Try inserting your own name where the *x*'s are in this rhyme:
"Xxxx, Xxxx, bo, bxxx, banana fanna fo fxxx, fee, fi
mo mxxx, Xxxx."
So, if your name were Jack, you would get:
"Jack, Jack, bo, back, banana fanna fo fack, fee, fi,
mo, mack, Jack."

————————LIKE WHICH ANIMAL?————————

Canine...Dog
Feline...Cat
Bovine..Cow
Ovine...Sheep
Porcine..Pig
Ursine...Bear
Equine...Horse
Vulpine...Fox
Leporine..Rabbit/hare
Anatine...Duck
Serpentine...Snake
Cervine...Deer
Delphine...Dolphin
Phocine..Seal
Elephantine...Elephant
Musteline..........Weasel, ferret, mink, stoat, etc.

————————INVENTIONS THAT DIDN'T MAKE IT————————

Thomas Edison's AUTOMATIC VOTE RECORDER (1869)—politicians didn't like it, perhaps because it was too accurate.

Henry Bessemer's ANTI-SEASICK BOAT (1875)—sailed straight into the pier at Calais because it could not be steered.

Sarah Guppy's ALL-IN-ONE BREAKFAST URN (1912)—could boil eggs and keep toast warm while boiling water for tea.

Bill Gates's TRAFF-O-DATA (1974)—could analyze the information collected by roadside car-counting devices.

Clive Sinclair's SINCLAIR C5 (1985)—a small, three-wheeled vehicle with a plastic body, an electric motor, and pedals for extra assistance going up hills.

————THE PREDICTIONS OF NOSTRADAMUS————

Michel de Notredame (Nostradamus) was a 16th-century French physician and astrologer who claimed to have visions of the future. He wrote a series of four-line verses in which he is believed to have predicted:

The death of King Henry II of France

Louis Pasteur's discovery of germs

The First World War

The rise of Hitler

The suspicious death of Pope John Paul I

The explosion of the space shuttle *Challenger*

The attacks on the Twin Towers in New York

——————THREE TERRIFYING PEOPLE——————

THE CANNIBAL
Hidden in a mile-deep remote cave in 17th-century Scotland, Sawney Beane and his family survived by ambushing travelers, robbing them—then eating them. It was 25 years before they were discovered, and when the horrified authorities found the cave it was filled with stolen jewelry and salted human remains hanging in rows along the cave walls.

THE IMPALER
Vlad Dracula, Prince of Wallachia (1431–1476), was the inspiration for Bram Stoker's novel about a blood-sucking vampire of the same name. He ruled through terror, and killed tens of thousands of his own people—mainly by publicly impaling them on stakes.

THE BLOOD BATHER
Elizabeth, Countess of Bathory (1560–1614), is said to have tortured and killed up to 2,000 girls and young women in Transylvania. She used a whip with articulated silver claws to tear the victims' flesh. According to legend she believed that bathing in their blood—and drinking the blood of the prettier ones—would keep her looking young and beautiful.

BIG BIRDS

Three ginormous birds—all flightless and now extinct.

THE ELEPHANT BIRD
Otherwise know as *Aepyornis*,
this huge bird from Madagascar
grew up to 9 ft. (2.7 m) tall, and
weighed as much as 992 lb.
(450 kg). It may have survived
until the arrival of
the first humans on the island,
and therefore gave rise to the
legend of the Roc.

THE GIANT DEMON
DUCK OF DOOM
Dromornis stirtoni from
Australia was even bigger,
reaching 9.8 ft. (3 m),
and weighing up to 1,102 lb. (500
kg). This is about the same
as a large horse.

THE GIANT MOA
This huge bird from New
Zealand was possibly the tallest
ever to walk the earth. It
reached 13 ft. (4 m) in height,
which is taller than most
elephants. It was more lightly
built, however, weighing up to
551 lb. (250 kg).

FUN HOUSES

Igloos • Wigwams • Houseboats
Tree houses • Yurts

HAIRY HUMANS

Hairs on the body:
1,400,000 – 5,000,000

Head hairs on a blonde:
150,000

Head hairs on a brunette:
100,000

Head hairs on a redhead:
90,000

Total length of hair grown in
one year:
7.5 mi. (12 km)

Number of hairs lost per day:
50 – 100

Longest hair ever:
16 ft. 11 in. (5.15 m)

Longest beard ever:
17 ft. 4.9 in. (5.33 m)

EXTREME IRONING

The weirdest places people have done their ironing are . . .

. . . across a 100-foot-wide gorge at Wolfberg Cracks
in South Africa.

. . . parachuting off the side of a cliff in the Australian
Blue Mountains complete with an iron, board, and laundry.

. . . on Mount Everest, at over 17,800 ft.

. . . while suspended underground at Alum Pot
in England's Yorkshire Dales.

. . . while running the London Marathon.

. . . underwater—especially when there are 50 people
doing it at once.

───────────TEN FAMOUS VOLCANOES───────────

Mount Etna, Sicily..Erupts almost constantly

Mount Fuji, Japan..Last erupted in 1707

Mauna Loa, Hawaii...........................World's largest erupting volcano

Mount Vesuvius, Italy...................................Destroyed Pompeii in 79 AD

Mount St. Helens, USA...Last erupted in 2005

Mount Pinatubo, Philippines...........................Erupted in 1991 and 1994

Yellowstone, USA.......................................Recent signs suggest activity

Popocatépetl, Mexico...Last erupted in 2005

Krakatoa, Indonesia.....................................Enormous eruption in 1883

Mount Kilimanjaro, Tanzania...............Ice Age snow cap has almost
completely melted away

───────────────WHICH DOORWAY?───────────────

You are trapped in a room. It is possible to get out but there's a snag. There are two doors through which you can leave, but while one leads to glorious freedom, the other will send you down into a bottomless pit from which there is no escape. And you don't know which door leads where. At each door stands a guard and you are allowed to ask one of them just one question to find out which door leads where. You know that one of the guards—you don't know which—invariably lies and the other always tells the truth. What should your question be?

"If you were the other guard, which door would you tell me leads to freedom?"
You then take the other exit.

| A baby in Florida was recently named |
| Truewilllaughinglifebuckyboomermanifestdestiny. |

──────MEDIEVAL TORTURE INSTRUMENTS──────

THUMBSCREW
A vice-like instrument that crushed the victim's thumbs.

THE PRESS
A board under which the victim was secured, and on top of which increasingly heavy weights were piled.

THE BOOT
A box-like iron device into which the victim's foot was thrust. Wedges were then pushed in to crush the ankle.

THE PENDULUM
A swinging blade, suspended over the victim, which was gradually lowered until the victim either confessed, or was cut in two.

RED-HOT PINCERS
The torturer would pinch the victim in increasingly sensitive areas until the required information was received.

THE RACK
A frame on which the victim was tied by the wrists and ankles, and then stretched.

THE IRON CHAIR
A chair in which the victim was tied. A fire was then lit beneath to heat it to scorching temperatures.

THE IRON MAIDEN
A coffin-shaped box lined with spikes. The victim was made to get into it, and then it was slowly pushed shut.

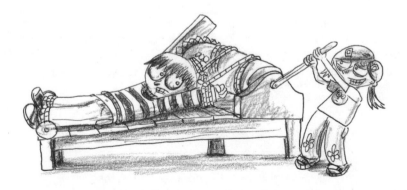

——FUNNY PLACE NAMES AROUND THE WORLD——

Boom, Belgium

Burrumbuttock, New South Wales, Australia

Camel Hump, Wyoming, USA

Ding Dong, Texas, USA

Hell, Cayman Islands

Kau Shi Wai, Hong Kong
(said to mean "village of dog poop" in Cantonese)

Louny, Czech Republic

Mumbles, Wales—to go with with Mutters in Austria?

Nasty, Hertfordshire, England

No Place, County Durham, England

Pratt's Bottom, London, England

Rottenegg, Austria

Shitagoo Lake, Quebec, Canada

Titlis, Switzerland

Tubbercurry, County Sligo, Ireland

Turda, Cluj, Romania

Wagga Wagga, New South Wales, Australia

Where Reynolds Cut The Firewood, Pitcairn Island

Wong Way, Singapore

Zzyzx, California, USA

The richest women in the world are Alice and Helen Walton, daughters of Sam Walton, founder of Wal-Mart, the world's largest retailer. They are worth $18 billion each.

---FOR YOUR ADDRESS BOOK---

The President of the United States of America
The White House
1600 Pennsylvania Avenue NW
Washington, DC 20500

Harry Potter
The Cupboard Under the Stairs
4 Privet Drive
Little Whinging
Surrey
Great Britain

The Queen of England
Buckingham Palace
London SW1A 1AA
Great Britain

Coca-Cola Headquarters
1 Coca-Cola Plaza
Atlanta, GA 30313

---HOW LONG DO YOUR CELLS LIVE?---

Stomach cells..Three days

Skin cells...Two to four weeks

Liver cells...Four to five months

Blood cells...Four to six months

Bone cells...Seven years

Brain cells...Can last a lifetime,
but you lose 10,000–100,000 per day

Luckily, the body produces over a billion cells per hour.

—————————THE 12 LABORS OF HERCULES—————————

Hercules was the son of a mortal woman and the ancient Greek god Zeus. Zeus's wife, the goddess Hera, was extremely jealous of Hercules and drove him to kill his own wife and children. As his penance Hercules was sentenced to perform 12 seemingly impossible labors. He became Greece's greatest hero.

1. Kill the monster lion of Nemea and bring back its skin.

2. Kill the many-headed Hydra, a swamp-dwelling monster.

3. Capture alive the Hind of Ceryneia, a deer with golden horns and bronze hoofs that was sacred to the goddess Artemis.

4. Capture alive the enormous boar that lived on Mount Erymanthus.

5. Clean (in one day) the 30 years' worth of filth left by thousands of cattle in the Augean stables.

6. Drive away a huge flock of man-eating birds.

7. Bring back, alive, the mad bull that was terrorizing Crete.

8. Capture the man-eating mares of Diomedes, King of Thrace.

9. Retrieve the girdle of Hippolyta, Queen of the Amazons.

10. Steal the oxen that belonged to the three-headed (or, some say, three-bodied) monster Geryon.

11. Fetch Hera's golden apples that were closely guarded by nymphs, the Hesperides, with the help of a many-headed dragon.

12. Bring back alive, and without using weapons, Cerberus, the ferocious three-headed dog that guarded the underworld.

2B OR NOT 2B?

The average pencil can draw a line about 35 mi. long (56 km), and can write up to 50,000 words. This is its story.

1560: A large deposit of graphite, a form of carbon, is discovered in Cumbria, England. The locals used it to mark their sheep.

It was thought to be a kind of lead and was named plumbago after the Latin name for lead, *plumbum*.

People began to wrap bits of sheepskin, string, or fabric around their plumbago sticks.

The concept spread to other countries, and in Italy they hit upon the idea of hollowing out sticks of juniper and sliding the plumbago in.

The writing tool became known as a pencil, from the Latin word for paintbrush, *peniculus*, which means "little tail."

Plumbago was renamed graphite, which comes from a Greek word meaning "to write."

1795: Nicholas Jacques Conté discovers that by mixing the graphite with clay he can vary the hardness, or darkness, of the pencil.

Today, pencils are graded H for "hardness" and
B for "blackness":

9H • 8H • 7H • 6H • 5H • 4H • 3H • 2H (no. 4) • H (no. 3)

F (no. 2½) • HB (no. 2)

B (no. 1) • 2B • 3B • 4B • 5B • 6B • 7B • 8B • 9B

---PIGPEN---

Pigpen is a secret code that is very easy to use, but impossible to read if you don't know how it works. First of all you need to write out the whole alphabet in two grids, as shown below:

Each letter is represented by the part of the "pigpen" that surrounds it. If it's the second letter in the box, then it has a dot in the middle.

So, this:

Translates as: Your fly is open.

---INSECT GRUB---

Three bee soup • Roasted grubs • Chocolate-covered locusts

Boiled silkworm larvae • Grasshoppers on toast

Mealworm and chocolate chip cookies

We also like deep-fried scorpions and tarantula sandwiches,

but those aren't insects. They're arachnids.

> You share your birthday with at least nine million other people on Earth.

97

"Jaws" is the most common name for a goldfish.

————————DAYS OF THE WEEK————————

English has roots in many languages. Most of the names of
the days of the week, for instance, come from Old Norse,
and are references to Norse gods.

Sunday	Day of the SUN
Monday	Day of the MOON
Tuesday	TYR's day (Tyr is the Norse god of war)
Wednesday	WODEN's day (Woden, or Odin, is the Norse god of wisdom)
Thursday	THOR's day (Thor is the Norse god of thunder)
Friday	FREYA's day (Freya is the Norse goddess of love)
Saturday	SATURN's day

———————————ABSENCE EXCUSE NOTES———————————

Please excuse Jennifer for missing school yesterday. We forgot to get the Sunday paper off the porch, and when we found it on Monday, we thought it was Sunday.

William was absent from school on May 8 because it was a national holiday in France and as we are part French we felt morally obliged to respect it here as well.

Flora was not in school yesterday because a badger stole her alarm clock. (Tonight we might let her sleep in the shed instead of under the rose bush.)

Edward will no longer be attending school as he has been offered a job with the secret service. Please do not ask any further questions or we may have to kill you.

———————————SUPER POWERS———————————

Flight • Invisibility • X-ray vision • Elasticity

Super-human strength • Super speed • Telekinesis

Shape-shifting • Force fields • Healing • Cryokinesis (ice)

Pyrokinesis (fire) • Telepathy / Mind reading

If a statue of a person on a horse has both front legs in the air, the person died in a battle; if the horse has one front leg in the air, the person died as a result of injuries received in battle; if the horse has all four legs on the ground, the person died of natural causes.

A doctor in the United States is developing a way to grow vaccines in bananas and other fruits, so that instead of having an injection all you'll have to do is eat the fruit!

————THEY SAY IT'S GOING TO RAIN IF . . .————

. . . frogs croak louder and longer than usual.

. . . dogs whine.

. . . roosters crow later in the day.

. . . birds fly lower to the ground and gather on tree branches and telephone wires.

. . . cows sit down in the fields to feed. Before a storm they run around the field with their tails high.

. . . bees and butterflies seem to disappear from the flower beds.

. . . fish jump out of the water to nip at low-flying insects.

————————OPPOSITES————————

mend/break	catch/throw
over/under	cover/expose
decrease/increase	compliment/insult
transparent/opaque	find/lose
clean up/mess up	buy/sell
send/receive	fake/genuine
give/take	rough/smooth

————WHY YOU DON'T WANT TO MESS———— WITH CREEPY CRAWLIES

Insects outnumber human beings a million to one.

The total weight of insects in the world is at least three times the combined weight of all other living creatures.

The global populations of ants, fly beetles, and springtails each outstrips the human race.

——MORE "FACTS" THAT ARE NOT TRUE——

Lemmings commit mass suicide.

Finland once banned Donald Duck because he doesn't wear pants.

The *Titanic* was described by her owners as "unsinkable."

Coca-Cola was originally green.

The rhyme "Ring Around the Rosie" is about the plague.

Ostriches bury their heads in the sand.

Tea contains more caffeine than coffee.

Eskimos have 400 words for snow.

——————CITY ANAGRAMS——————

Copenhagen	Hence, a pong!
Buenos Aires	Senior abuse
Los Angeles	Sells an ego
Edinburgh	Ugh! Inbred
Amsterdam	Edam, trams
Barcelona	Able acorn
New York	Worn key
Calcutta	Act a cult
Adelaide	A dead lie

---------------------------- IMPOSTERS ----------------------------

PRINCESS ANASTASIA a.k.a. Anna Anderson moved from Berlin to the United States when she married the American John Manahan. She claimed throughout her life that she was the sole survivor of the Russian royal family, murdered in 1918. She died in 1981, some ten years before DNA testing proved that she was not Anastasia.

TUESDAY LOBSANG RAMPA was famous for his books about spirituality and his childhood in Tibet, and became a lama (a Buddhist monk). When he was found actually to be an Englishman named Cyril Hoskins, he insisted that his body had been taken over by the lama one Tuesday, and went on writing his books. He died in 1981.

THE TICHBORNE CLAIMANT traveled from Australia to England under an assumed name in 1866 and duped Lady Tichborne into believing he was her long-lost son and heir to the Tichborne baronetcy.

GEORGE PSALMANAZAR fooled people all over 18th-century Europe into believing he was a cannibal prince from an exotic eastern land, publishing books about his native country and even teaching at Oxford University, England.

PRINCESS CARABOO enjoyed many weeks of celebrity in 1817 as a princess from "Javasu" who'd been kidnapped by pirates and had escaped. Her fun was spoiled when she was recognized as Mary Baker, a servant girl.

------- HIGHEST-EARNING FICTIONAL CHARACTERS -------

1. Mickey Mouse
2. Winnie the Pooh
3. Frodo Baggins
4. Harry Potter
5. Nemo

6. Yu-Gi-Oh!
7. SpongeBob SquarePants
8. Spider-Man
9. Wolverine (X-Men)
10. Pikachu (Pokémon)

THE SIGNS OF MADNESS

The first sign of madness is talking to yourself.

The second sign of madness is growing hair on your palms.

The third sign of madness is looking for hair on your palms.

CARD TRICK

Take all 13 cards from one suit, e.g., hearts, and secretly arrange them in this order:

Queen, four, ace, eight, king, two, seven, five, ten, jack, three, six, nine.

Hold all 13 cards in a pile facedown with the queen on the top and say to your audience, "A-C-E spells ace." As you say each letter, take the card from the top of the stack and place it at the bottom, but as you say the last letter, take the card from the top and place it faceup on the table, showing your audience it's the ace. Now you can count all the way up to the king in this manner ("T-W-O spells two"; "T-H-R-E-E spells three"; "F-O-U-R spells four"; etc.) and amaze your friends as you spell out the correct card every time!

———————— SAY WHAT YOU SEE ————————

BAD wolf

Big bad wolf

Y
N
N
U
S

Sunny side up

MY ~~HEART~~

Cross my heart

S  1

Back to square one

YOURANTSPANTS

Ants in your pants

HEAD
HEELS

Head over heels in love

SHUT

SIT

Shut up and sit down

WISH

Wish upon a star

———————HOTTEST, COLDEST, DRIEST, WETTEST———————

HIGHEST TEMPERATURE RECORDED
On September 13, 1922, the temperature in Al'Aziziyah, Libya, reached a scorching 135.9°F (57.7°C).

LONGEST HOT SPELL
For 162 consecutive days (October 30, 1923–April 7, 1924) in Marble Bar, Western Australia, the temperature never dropped below 100°F (37.8°C).

LOWEST TEMPERATURE RECORDED
On July 21, 1983, the temperature in Vostok, Antarctica, plummeted to -128.6°F (-89.2°C).

LOWEST AVERAGE ANNUAL MEAN TEMPERATURE
At Plateau Station in Antarctica the average temperature is -70°F (-56.7°C).

DRIEST REGION
In some parts of Antarctica it hasn't rained at all for over two million years.

WETTEST PLACE
In Cherrapunji, India, there is approximately 500 in. (1,270 cm) of rain per year.

LARGEST HAILSTONE
A ginormous hailstone measuring 7 in. (17.8 cm) in diameter and 18.74 in. (47.6 cm) in circumference landed in Nebraska on June 22, 2003.

Your brain uses 13 percent less energy when you sit watching television than when you do nothing at all.

A swarm of locusts covering an area of 2,000 square miles crossed the Red Sea in 1889. It was estimated to weigh 500,000 tons and contain 250 thousand million locusts.

THE OLYMPIC GAMES

776 BC First Olympic Games held at Olympia, Greece. It was a one-day event consisting of a 200-meter race.

472 BC The games are increased to five days, to allow for new activities such as boxing and wrestling.

1896 The modern Olympics, a revival of the Olympian Games, are held in Athens, largely thanks to the French sportsman Baron Pierre de Coubertin. The event continues to be held every four years.

1924 The Winter Olympics, held in the same year as the Summer Olympics, are added to the Olympic calendar.

1994 The International Olympic Committee decides to hold the Winter and Summer Olympics on alternate even years.

The Olympic motto is "Citius, Altius, Fortius"—"Swifter, Higher, Stronger." The Olympic symbol is a white background with five interlocking circles colored blue, yellow, black, green, and red. At least one of those colors (including white) appears in the national flag of every country.

—WHAT'S BLACK AND WHITE AND RED ALL OVER?—

A newspaper • A sunburnt nun • An embarrassed zebra

A penguin with chicken pox • A Dalmatian holding its breath

A vampire who's spilled his dinner on himself

A skunk in a blender

FAMOUS GHOSTS

THE WHISTLESTOP GHOST

A bearded man in a gray coat who has haunted a train-station café in Waitakere, New Zealand, since the 1920s. The mysterious figure is said to be a man who was hit by a passing train.

TRIANON PALACE

On August 10, 1901, two English women seemed to slip back in time while visiting the palace at Versailles in France. They felt a strange sense of gloom and loneliness, and then encountered a series of figures in 18th-century dress. They later discovered that the grounds were said to be haunted by Marie Antoinette and her court, and that a bridge they crossed had been destroyed many years earlier.

LA LLORONA

The ghost of a Mexican woman who fell in love with a nobleman and killed her children so that she could be with him (he didn't much fancy having a load of kids to look after). She then became so grief-stricken that she killed herself. To this day she roams the land, weeping and looking for her lost children.

THE ROSENHEIM POLTERGEIST

From 1967 to 1969 a lawyer's office in Germany was affected by strange phenomena witnessed by over 40 people. Lights flickered, bulbs fell out of their sockets, telephone calls were cut off, pictures rotated on the walls, and filing cabinets moved by themselves.

————————MIXING COLOR————————

PAINT	LIGHT
red + yellow = orange	red + green = yellow*
yellow + blue = green	green + blue = cyan*
blue + red = purple	blue + red = magenta*
red + yellow + blue = brown	red + green + blue = white*

*With colored lights, what's actually happening is that by using more than one wavelength of light, you can trick your brain into thinking it sees a color that isn't really there.

————————THE FATE OF THE CHILDREN IN————————
CHARLIE AND THE CHOCOLATE FACTORY

AUGUSTUS GLOOP, in his greed to devour chocolate, falls in the chocolate river and is sucked up into a pipe to be taken to the strawberry fudge room.

VIOLET BEAUREGARDE disregards Mr. Wonka's warning and eats an experimental meal in chewing-gum form; when she gets to the dessert, blueberry pie, she turns into a giant blueberry and is taken away to have the juice squeezed out of her.

VERUCA SALT tries to take a trained nut-testing squirrel, but the squirrels test her and she is thrown down the bad-nut chute into a disgusting rubbish dump in the basement.

MIKE TEAVEE disobeys Mr. Wonka and tries to send himself across the room via television. He miniaturizes himself in the process.

CHARLIE BUCKET, because he isn't greedy or naughty or vain or addicted to television, is the only remaining child, and Mr. Wonka hands the factory over to him.

FINGER FUN

Make a bet with a friend that if you point to one of their fingers and ask them to wiggle it, they'll wiggle the wrong one. If they accept the bet, tell them to put their arms out and cross them at the wrists. They should then turn their palms together and interlock their fingers. Now ask them to bring their hands in toward their stomach, and continue moving their hands around and upward until their interlocked fingers are on top. Now point to one of their fingers (don't actually touch it) and see if they know which one to wiggle. The third and fourth finger on each hand is the hardest to figure out, so start with those if you want to win the bet.

WHAT TEACHERS REALLY MEAN

"Good morning."
Please, don't throw anything.

"What page are we on?"
I've completely forgotten what I've been teaching you.

"We're going to work in groups today, then you
can present your ideas to the class."
I'm too tired to teach—you do the work.

─────────WHY IS THE SKY BLUE?─────────

Light is made up of different colors that we can see separately when we look at a rainbow. Some of these colors travel through air and dust quite easily, but blue light gets bounced around by molecules of air. So when you look up at the sky, you are really seeing miles and miles of blue light in the air. The sea appears to be blue because it reflects the sky.

─────────EVERYDAY INVENTIONS─────────

Wooden coat hangers...........Thomas Jefferson, c. 1790

Tea bags.............................Thomas Sullivan, 1908

Frozen food...................Clarence Birdseye, 1925

Ballpoint pens...............................László Biró, 1938

Velcro............................Georges de Mestral, 1948

Computer games....................A. S. Douglas, 1952

Digital wristwatch.............Sir Clive Sinclair, 1976

CDs.............................Toshi Tada Doi, 1979

World Wide Web............................Tim Berners-Lee, 1989

COUNTRIES WITH THE MOST TRACTORS PER PERSON

Slovenia

Ireland

Austria

Yugoslavia

Finland

ANNOYING THINGS TEACHERS ALWAYS SAY

"I don't care who started it."

"Something's obviously very funny, so why don't you share it with the rest of us?"

"This is for your benefit, so please wake up."

"Honestly, it's like talking to a brick wall sometimes."

"I'd expect that kind of behavior from her, but really, I'm surprised at you."

"If you're so clever, why don't you come up here and teach?"

"Would you do that at home?"

"Come on. We're waiting."

MUSIC GENRES

Classical

Jazz

Folk

R & B/Soul

Rock

Country

Electronic

Dance

Reggae

Pop

Easy Listening

World

Latin

Opera

Blues

New Age

──────── NAMES OF THE MONTHS ────────

The word *month* comes from *moon*, because months were once measured from full moon to full moon (about 29 days). In ancient Roman times there were just ten months in the year, and the first was March:

March	Named after Mars, the Roman god of war
April	From the Latin *aperire*, meaning "to open"
May	Named after Maia, goddess of spring
June	Named after Juno, queen of Roman gods
Quintilis	Latin for "fifth"
Sextilis	Latin for "sixth"
September	Latin for "seventh"
October	Latin for "eighth"
November	Latin for "ninth"
December	Latin for "tenth"

Then, in the seventh century BC, January and February were added at the beginning of the year. This is why our ninth month is called the seventh (September), and so on.

January	Named after the Roman god of gateways
February	From the religious purification ritual *februum* that took place that month. The festival was named after Februus, the Etruscan god of the dead and of purification.

In 44 BC, Julius Caesar decided a month should be named after him:

July	Used to be Quintilis, renamed after Julius Caesar

Augustus Caesar thought this was a great idea . . .

August	Used to be Sextilis, renamed after Augustus Caesar

———SEVEN SPELLS FROM HARRY POTTER———

Alohomora—to open a locked door

Colloportus—to seal a door (with a squelch)

Expecto Patronum—to conjure up a Patronus
(used to drive away Dementors, etc.)

Impedimenta—to stop or slow something down

Incendio—to start a fire

Petrificus Totalus—to turn someone to stone

Tarantallegra—to cause someone to dance madly

———————HOW TO FAKE A SMILE———————

Because smiling releases endorphins, even faking a smile can improve a person's mood. There are different types of smiles— "felt" smiles, which are explosions of joy and happiness, and "social" smiles (said to number 18 different kinds)—smiles of greeting, thanks, reassurance, etc. People can differentiate between felt and social smiles; in felt smiles the muscles that raise the cheekbones also contract, making the eyes crease up, and the eyebrows dip slightly. Smiling is infectious—smile at people and the likelihood is that they'll smile back.

———————————THE CHAIR OF TRUTH———————————

To play this trick on a friend, place a sponge soaked with water on a chair that has a slatted seat (one that will allow water to drain through). Cover the sponge up with a towel and drape towels and cushions all over the chair to disguise what you have done. Finally, place an empty tin upside down underneath the chair.

Ask your friend to stand next to the Chair of Truth while you ask him or her some questions. After each answer, look at the chair and say, "The Chair of Truth agrees that you have answered honestly."

Now ask your friend the question: "What is the last thing you do each night before you go to bed?" Most people will probably answer that they clean their teeth, or read a book, or have a drink of water. Look at the chair and say, "The Chair of Truth says that you are lying. You must sit on the chair so that I can know the truth."

When your friend sits on the chair the water will drain from the sponge through the slats and make a loud dripping noise on the tin beneath.

"The Chair of Truth says that the last thing you do before you go to sleep at night is go to the bathroom."

———————————RABBIT OR DUCK?———————————

Each foot has over 250,000 sweat glands, and in a day one foot can produce more than a pint of sweat! The smell is caused not by the sweat but by bacteria that eat the sweat and excrete strong-smelling waste. In the damp cozy darkness of our socks and shoes, these microbes feast away merrily and the more sweat the smellier. Armpits are another nice, warm, cozy, sweaty place for bacteria.

──────A ROMAN BANQUET SET MENU──────

DRINK
Spiced wine
Water
(Please note that slaves will frequently refill your cup.)

STARTER
Gustatio, consisting of sea urchins with spices, oil, and egg sauce
Jellyfish and eggs
Milk-fed snails fried in oil

MAIN COURSE
Deer roasted with onion sauce
Dates, raisins, and honey
Boiled flamingo in a spicy sauce
Roast boar stuffed with small birds
Sausages and vegetables
Baked dormice stuffed with pork and pine kernels
Roast parrot with dates
Jugs of *garum* and *liquamen* (sauces made from fermented fish)

DESSERT
Dates with almonds and honey
Roses baked in pastry
Dates stuffed with nuts and pine kernels, fried in honey

——TEN GRAND PRIX FORMULA 1 CHAMPIONS——

1. Mika Hakkinen (McLaren-Mercedes) 1998, 1999
2. Damon Hill (Williams-Renault) 1996
3. Niki Lauda (Ferrari) 1975, 1977; (McLaren-TAG/Porsche) 1984
4. Nigel Mansell (Williams-Renault) 1992
5. Nelson Piquet (Brabham-Ford/Cosworth) 1981; (Brabham BMW) 1983; (Williams-Honda) 1987
6. Alain Prost (McLaren-TAG/Porsche) 1985, 1986; (McLaren-Honda) 1989; (Williams-Renault) 1993
7. Keke Rosberg (Williams-Ford/Cosworth) 1982
8. Michael Schumacher (Benetton-Ford) 1994; (Benetton-Renault) 1995; (Ferrari) 2000, 2001, 2002, 2003, 2004
9. Ayrton Senna (McLaren-Honda) 1988, 1990, 1991
10. Jacques Villeneuve (Williams-Renault) 1997

In a recent survey 54 percent of people said they fold toilet paper neatly to wipe; 35 percent bunch it up into a ball. What the remaining 11 percent do is not recorded.

———THE FIVE DEADLIEST PLACES ON EARTH———

TAKLAMAKAN DESERT

Located in northwest China, farther from the ocean than any other place on earth, it receives almost no rain. It is boiling hot in summer, prone to dust storms, and is used as a nuclear weapons testing ground.

ANNAPURNA MOUNTAIN

With more than five avalanches a day, this mountain in Nepal has the highest death toll of any climbing peak in the world.

SHARK ALLEY

Just off the coast of Cape Town in South Africa, this channel between two islands is infested with sharks who sometimes mistake humans for their usual diet of seals.

LA PAZ TO COROICO ROAD

The 40-mile-long trail in the mountains of Bolivia is also known as the "Road of Death." It is very narrow, very steep, and runs along the edge of a deep valley. There is a fatal accident there about once every two weeks.

AMBOPATA RESERVE

One of the most remote parts of the Amazon jungle, it is home to the wandering spider (the most deadly spider in the world), stinging ants, killer caterpillars, deadly vipers, skin-crawling bicho worms, piranha fish, and many other death-inducing creatures.

———LANGUAGES OF WIDER COMMUNICATION———

Some people believe that an international language might solve world problems that are caused by misunderstandings of communication. The most successful international languages are:

ENGLISH: Widely spoken, and is the international language used by airplane pilots.

ESPERANTO: An invented language with straightforward grammar and simple pronunciation.

LOGLAN: A laboratory-created language designed to be easy for anyone from any culture to learn.

ART MOVEMENTS

Classical	Fauvism
Renaissance	Modernism
Mannerism	Expressionism
Baroque	Cubism
Rococo	Dadaism
Romanticism	Surrealism
Pre-Raphaelite	Abstraction
Symbolism	Pop Art
Realism	Op Art
Impressionism	Postmodernism

HOMEMADE INVISIBLE INK

Mix one spoon of baking powder with 1 to 2 spoons of cold water.

Dip a toothpick or cotton swab in the mixture and use it to write your message on a piece of white paper.

Wait for the ink to dry.

Hold the paper up to a light bulb and the message will appear.

Alternatively, paint the paper with purple grape juice to reveal the secret message.

MOONS OF JUPITER

Metis	Io	Leda	Ananke
Adrastea	Europa	Himalia	Carme
Amalthea	Ganymede	Lysithea	Pasiphaë
Thebe	Callisto	Elara	Sinope

UNIDENTIFIED FLYING OBJECTS

Theories as to what UFOs could be include:

Aircraft or airships • Weather balloons • Kites • Parachutes

Insect swarms • Clouds so high they reflect the sun at night

The Northern Lights • Meteor showers or comets

Ball lightning • Secret military operations

SOME INTERESTING SIGHTINGS:

Norfolk, UK, December 26—28, 1980: men from a Royal Air Force base in the area saw an airborne object and strange bright lights. The next day investigators found broken branches and three small circular depressions in the soil.

Minsk, USSR (now Russia), September 7, 1984: the pilots of a Soviet airliner reported seeing a strange, brightly glowing form that followed their path for several minutes, changing shape repeatedly. A second flight crew traveling in the opposite direction also reported seeing a glowing object. A Soviet missile was being launched at the time—but in order to protect military secrets, Soviet officials denied the missile's existence.

Brussels, Belgium, March 30, 1990: two F-16 fighter pilots were sent to intercept an unexplained object detected by radar. It was night. They locked their radar on the object, but it sped away; they chased it for 75 minutes, then lost it.

TANGRAMS

Tangrams were first created in ancient China. A square is divided into seven pieces (as shown). The aim is then to combine the seven shapes to create images or symbols, typically of weird and wonderful people, animals, or objects.

——THE LONGEST PLACE NAMES IN THE WORLD——

Krung Thep Mahanakhon Amon Rattanakosin Mahinthara Ayuthaya Mahadilok Phop Noppharat Ratchathani Burirom Udomratchaniwet Mahasathan Amon Piman Awatan Sathit Sakkathattiya Witsanukam Prasit

At 21 words/168 letters long, this ceremonial name for Thailand's capital city Krung Thep, or, as we know it, Bangkok, is the longest place name in the world. It means:

"The city of angels, the great city, the eternal jewel city, the impregnable city of God Indra, the grand capital of the world endowed with nine precious gems, the happy city, abounding in an enormous Royal Palace that resembles the heavenly abode where reigns the reincarnated god, a city given by Indra and built by Vishnukarn."

The longest single-word place name belongs to a town in New Zealand called

Tetaumatawhakatangihangakoauaotamateaurehaeaturipukapihim- aungahoronukupokaiwhenuaakitanarahu

It is 92 letters long and means:

"The brow of the hill [or place], where Tamatea, the man with the big knees, who slid [down], climbed [up] and swallowed mountains, [to travel the land], [and is] known as the Land Eater, played [on] his [nose] flute to his loved one."

——————GROUND-TO-AIR CODE——————

MESSAGE	CODE SYMBOL
We need help	V
We need a doctor	X
Yes	Y
No	N
It should be safe to land here	△
We've gone this way	→

---FIVE FAMOUS HOAXES---

THE CARDIFF GIANT
(New York, 1869)
Workmen found the fossilized remains of a huge man buried in the grounds of a farm. Eventually, two men admitted that they had made the giant bones out of a calcium-based substance called gypsum.

THE COTTINGLEY FAIRIES
(Yorkshire, England, 1917)
Elsie Wright (15) and her cousin Frances Griffiths (10) fooled the world with their photographs of fairies. It was not until 1983 that they explained they had cut the fairies out of a book!

PILTDOWN MAN
(Sussex, England, 1912)
Scientists were presented with the fossil remains of what was claimed to be the "missing link" between man and ape. It was not until 1953 that modern testing methods showed it to be a very clever patchwork of human skull, orangutan jawbone, and elephant and hippo teeth. The hoaxer has never been identified.

HITLER'S DIARIES
(Germany, 1983)
A reputable German journal announced its scoop—62 volumes of Adolf Hitler's diaries—for which they had paid an enormous sum. In their excitement, they had missed a lot of historical innacuracies and failed to carry out proper tests—it soon became apparent that the diaries were a hoax carried out by a dealer in documents.

THE AMITYVILLE HORROR
(New York, 1974)
George and Katy Lutz moved into a house in which a man had shot his parents and four siblings dead. A month later they moved out again, and published the story of their experiences in the house—complete with tales of swarms of flies, demonic cats, ghostly apparitions, green slime . . . the lot. The couple made a great deal of money out of it, then admitted in 1979 that they had concocted the whole story.

Time flies like an arrow, fruit flies like bananas.

——FIVE WAYS TO DE-SMELL YOUR SNEAKERS——

A couple of drops of peppermint oil.

Fill a sock with cat litter (preferably unused) and leave in the sneaker overnight.

Put a fabric-softener sheet in the bottom of the sneaker.

Dust the inside of the sneaker with baby powder.

Leave a few unused tea bags in the shoe for two days.

——————CELEBRITY DRAGONS——————

Draco..........................Teams up with the dragonslayer in *Dragonheart*

Dragon...Falls in love with Donkey in *Shrek*

Horntail Dragon........Stars in *Harry Potter and the Goblet of Fire*

Puff..The magic dragon from the song

Smaug...In *The Hobbit* by J. R. R. Tolkien

Norbert.....................Hagrid's baby dragon in *Harry Potter and the Sorcerer's Stone*

--------WHAT ANIMALS SAY--------

SHEEP
"baa" (English)
"bee hee" (Croatian)
"maeh" (Danish)
"bee-bee" (Slovenian)

PIGS
"gron-gron" (French)
"ha-roo" (Russian)
"oot-oot" (Thai)
"moo-moo" (Japanese)
"oink" (English)

DOGS
"ouaf-ouaf" (French)
"brippi brippi" (Italian)
"gong gong" (Indonesian)
"bahk-bahk" (Thai)
"wan-wan" (Japanese)
"gahf-gahft" (Russian)
"wang wang" (Chinese)

COWS
"oo-ah" (Thai)
"meuh" (French)
"moo" (English)

ROOSTERS
"cock-a-doodle-doo" (English)
"kickerikie" (German)
"cocorico" (French)

CATS
"neow" (Japanese)
"miaou" (French)
"meow" (English)
"mao" (Thai)

BEES
"buzz-buzz" (English)
"bhon-bhon" (Bengali)
"wing-wing" (Korean)

--------WHAT BLUE MEANS--------

Life • Spirituality • Loyalty • Fidelity • Peace • Tranquillity

Sadness • Depression • Mourning • Dreaminess

Reliability • Authority

124

————RAINBOWS——THE TRUTH AND THE LIES————

TRUTH: A RAINBOW IS BENT LIGHT
Sunlight passes through drops of rainwater, which act like little prisms and bend the light and then reflect it back from the surface of the drops. The amount of bending, known as refraction, differs for light of different colors—red light bends the least and violet light bends the most.

LIE: THERE IS GOLD AT THE END OF THE RAINBOW
Rainbows are in fact circular, and therefore don't have "ends."

TRUTH: ROY G. BiV
This is a mnemonic to help you remember the colors of the rainbow: Red, Orange, Yellow, Green, Blue, Violet.

LIE: THERE ARE SEVEN COLORS IN THE RAINBOW
There are really only six—indigo is just the blue fading into the violet, but Sir Isaac Newton, who investigated light and color, was a superstitious man, and believed seven to be a lucky number.

TRUTH: A HIGH SUN CAUSES A LOW RAINBOW
When the sun is more than 42 degrees above the horizon, no rainbow is visible.

————————NAME THAT BAND————————

COLDPLAY – originally called Starfish. Friends of theirs were in a band called Coldplay, but later disbanded and let them have the name. The original band got the name from a collection of poems by Philip Horky.

FOO FIGHTERS – Dave Grohl was fascinated by UFOs. He named his new band after an expression used in the Second World War by pilots to describe the alien-looking fireballs they sometimes saw over Germany.

NICKELBACK – The bass player once worked at Starbucks, and spent many days saying, "Here's your nickel back."

U2 – named after the American U-2 spy plane.

—————————YOU ARE NOW . . .—————————

Informed
Knowledgeable
Clued-up
Tuned-in
Savvy
With-it
Learned
Enlightened